The Rediscovery of Prayer

Other Books by the Author

HAPPY THOSE WHO BELIEVE

SPIRITUALITY OF THE SACRAMENTS
Doctrine and Practice for Today

The Rediscovery of Prayer

BERNARD BRO, O.P.

Translated by John Morriss

alba house books

CANFIELD, OHIO 44406

248.3

Original title: APPRENDRE A PRIER,
published by Les Editions du Cerf, Paris.

The nihil obstat and imprimatur are official
declarations that a book or pamphlet is free of
doctrinal or moral error. No implication is contained therein that those who have granted the
nihil obstat and imprimatur agree with the
contents, opinions or statements expressed.

Nihil Obstat:
    JOHN A. GOODWINE, J.C.D., Censor Librorum

Imprimatur:
    ★ TERENCE J. COOKE, D.D., V.G.

Library of Congress Catalog Card Number: 72-9578

Printed and bound in the U.S.A.

CONTENTS

PREFACE

Two statements in the Gospel summarize the entire development of our prayer life: the request of the Apostles — "Lord, teach us how to pray," and the complaint of Christ — "Could you not watch one hour with me?"

We will never learn completely how to pray or fully understand that only the Spirit of God can intercede and call out for us — we who ignore what is good for us. And yet, our concern for God will never equal the concern God has for us. Although we think we are generous, when the time comes we always have an alibi available to avoid praying.

We learn very early in life not to be too sure of ourselves. Every kind of illusion regarding prayer is indeed a serious one. What value do our lives have when we no longer yearn for God?

Too often we try to find a remedy for our delinquency and lethargy in formulas or bits of advice that are of value for only a short while. Basically, however, the real difficulties and objections still remain with us; we are still not convinced that prayer is necessary. More specifically, we are unable to reconcile it with our faith. The following pages are intended to help us in this matter.

I

WHY PRAY?

"Before they call, I will answer."
— Isaiah 65:24

"Without me, you can do nothing"

IS PRAYER NECESSARY?

WHEN we approach the mysteries of the Christian faith, we should do so with a sense of fidelity, courage and lucidity. Frequently, however, we remain in a middle-of-the-road position and have little desire to cast light on our illusions and contradictory positions.

This is certainly true of prayer. And yet, we have no desire of clarifying this situation. On the one hand, we can think of numerous objections made against prayer, and yet we try to avoid them as much as possible. On the other, we are conscious of our need of God — an ineradicable need — and know that we possess the truth, and are therefore happy, only when we are with God, only insofar as we accept a dialogue with him. Instead of yielding to these objections, let us try to use them as a way of gaining access to the mystery. In this way, they will help us to overcome the contradictions that we otherwise fear. Let us begin by summarizing them:

First, the *lack of time*. Our everyday schedules are overcrowded. Why invite us to pray when it will take up more of such precious time? Next, *fatigue*. Why a new fatigue, and above all an additional intellectual tension? Finally, the *complexity of this interior effort.* Why strain our desire for simplicity by the search for dialogue with God, a dialogue that proves itself every day as a difficult, complicated one? We are frightened by such questions, and yet, if they pertain to us and can be of value, they can serve as a guideline for our study and direct it toward essentials. But for this to happen, we must pass beyond a simple psychological examination and go much deeper.

There is, however, a more fundamental objection; beyond the lack of time, fatigue and impatience, there is a further problem that continues to gnaw at us, although it is often not expressed: *Isn't our prayer useless*? Here we are skillful in preserving a state of illusion, and even take advantage of the situation by saying it is all part of the mystery of God.

If I believe what I am told about God, he is perfect and immutable in the fullness of his knowledge and force. If God is God, he is sufficient unto himself. In that case, of what use will my prayer be? Thus, the real objection is a two-sided one: If God is God, he knows everything; I have nothing to tell him, and so what's the sense of repeating my needs to him? If God is God, he does not change, and therefore what's the use of asking him to intervene in my life?

GOD KNOWS EVERYTHING

"For your Father knows what you need before you ask him"

It is true, prayer does not "help" God. It is "useless" to him, and our Lord has told us so himself: "But in praying, do not multiply words, as the Gentiles do; for they think that by saying a great deal, they will be heard. So do not be like them; for your Father knows what you need before you ask him" (Matthew 6:7-8). *God knows better than we what is good for us*, and thus prayer and the continued use of prayer is of no use to him but to us. Actually, if God knows everything, it is up to us to learn, for we are never sufficiently aware of our ignorance of the nature and extent of our real needs.

Impatience with One's Limitations

We can give a number of descriptions of what an adolescent is, but perhaps the best definition is that of someone who has not yet experienced his limitations, and therefore has not had to accept them. By this test, a human being becomes a man and thereby evaluates himself. Now, prayer is the *pedagogy of God* during the course of this experience, which is one of the most common and profound experiences of our life. Prayer helps us by making us conscious of our limitations.

This is a test that every man is called to make. A "test," because such an experience is always difficult, painful and inevitably realized in the course of failures: failure in our intellectual study, our feelings, our actions. It is difficult to love and to be loved as one would like. It is painful to realize that there are whole areas in the life of the mind that will never be revealed. Every man, one day or another, becomes aware of his poverty as a creature. And since this experience is a crushing one, the natural temptation is therefore distractions, or, as Pascal said, *diversions*. There is an "impatience with one's limitations," a natural temptation that urges us to flee before such limitations. We experience a fear in coming face to face with them, and this fear arises again and again inside us. Distractions, therefore, appear as the opposite of prayer, a refusal of our real condition, an evasion of it in favor of illusion, dream, mirage (recall man's pursuit of different kinds of drunkenness: evasion by the flesh, art, sports, etc.).

However, the first moment of true prayer occurs in the experience and awareness of one's limitations. We do not know what our real needs are, and we must learn them all over again each day. In this sense, prayer has the value of pedagogy, it is the great pedagogy of God. While evasion and distractions draw us away from the road to real happiness, prayer brings us back to what is most authentic in man's quest for happiness. "The truth will set you free." Prayer makes us free; it preserves what is most fragile and most precious in us: the integrity of our desire, that desire which, in final analysis, is nothing but the need for God. This is what prayer preserves in us, and must teach us every day, this need for God, which is the distinctive, most profound trait that separates man from the animals. Man is the only being who turns to God to obtain what is lacking for his own fulfillment.

To Pray Is Not Easy

Is prayer always spontaneous in us? Is it not normal to try to avoid what is disagreeable, especially the discovery of one's own inadequacies? Is not the refusal to recognize one's own limitations a proof of adolescence? See, on the contrary, the attitude of "men of faith," men "according to the heart of God": Abraham, David, Jeremias, who were aware of their own inadequacy and who recognized their inabilities right away. Nevertheless, were they not sometimes led to this attitude against their instinctive desires, which tend *per se* to leave people in a state of illusion about themselves? See, for example, the life of Moses: Exodus 2:11-15 and 3:11-12; 4:10; 5:22-23.

Does not the awareness of our limitations already imply a call from God? Does not prayer then appear as man's response to the invitation made to him by God?

This call from God often takes disturbing forms. See, in the case of Agar, the jealousy of men and the flight into the desert: Genesis 21:8-21. See also Elias: I Kings 19:1f.; or the exile of the people: Baruch 2:30-3:8.

Is not the true call of God almost always made in the discovery of our inadequacies? See, for example, the story of the Prodigal Son (read again Luke 15). The father does not have any meaning for his son except when the latter actually experiences his own inability to achieve happiness by himself and organize his life through his own efforts.

What attitude do we have regarding such an experience? Compare, in the Bible, the attitude of Saul and that of David (Saul: I Samuel 13:9-14; 14:36-46; 18:8-12; 18:20-29; 28:7-15; and, on the contrary, David: II Samuel 6:17-29; 12:13-23; 15:23-26; 18:1-19:2). Both men fall victim to weakness, but for Saul, this is only a new occasion for pride and self-sufficiency, and after breaking with God, he will try to reconcile himself with God and win him over at any price, even by magic. For David, however, it is an opportunity to really discover God; he does not try "to win his favor" by himself, to save himself on his own strength, but he finds out that he draws closer to God when he accepts the fact that he needs him.

When God leads a man to a state of poverty, is this not always to bring about an increase of love? "But in the land of their captivity they shall have a change of heart; they shall know that I, the Lord, am their God" (cf. Baruch 2:29-35). Is this not the meaning of all "exile"? In your own life, what are the forms of this exile and this state of poverty? Can we discover, beneath the negative and paradoxical sense of all this, the invitation that is made to us to recognize the divine presence?

God Needs Men

"The truth will set you free." This fact is sometimes difficult to accept, and the pedagogy which uses the experience of our poverty is painful since poverty always crushes us. But prayer does more than make us aware of our limitations: it transforms that part of our life that weighs us down and crushes us, and changes the nature of this poverty. Actually, our life with God is the same as any life based on love: it can continue to exist only when each person accepts the fact that he needs the other. This is the second achievement of prayer: after bringing us to accept our limitations and making us aware of our real need, *it transforms that need, that deficiency, that poverty, into a dependence upon someone else.* Love will not rest until it achieves its goal: to share everything in order to bring about the unity toward which it tends. To achieve this, love demands reciprocity, need of another and the mutual consciousness of this need. We know very well how a yearning for someone else, a separation, unhappiness, all spring from a refusal to reciprocate. On the other hand, we know that all the happiness proper to love arises from the voluntary acceptance of the fact that one person needs another: no longer being able to do without the other, both people now strive to do everything together. *Love needs the need of another.* It nourishes itself and continues to exist on the awareness of this need within itself. God likewise needs our need.

Thus, the poverty which before crushed us now becomes, through prayer, a source of wealth, by which we gain possession of the heart of God. To refuse to recognize one's own poverty, is not to recognize God; it means refusing to allow him to be God for us. For me, God is God only when I accept the fact that I need him. Furthermore, God does not want to give us what we are lacking, although he knows what we need, until we have first asked him for it. Just as a mother, at four o'clock in the afternoon, knows very well that her child is hungry, that it is time for a snack, she will wait for that insignificant little act, the gesture that will tell her that her child is happy to have to ask her for something, to need her. Thus our poverty becomes a source of wealth, provided that we are conscious every day that *I am in the night, but I am no longer in prison, I am no longer alone.* Here, the repetition of prayer is seen as something necessary. The experience of our limitations is actually too painful for us not to want to run away from it, as long as we have not learned to look at it in its true light.

Agar, sent away to the desert with her son, laments and prays: "Let me not see my child die." The angel of God appears and comforts her: "What is the matter, Agar? Fear not; for God has heard the boy's cry in this plight of his. Rise up, take the boy, be assured in his regard; for I will make him a great nation" (Genesis 21:16-17). "Our Father who is in heaven knows better than you what you need." God heard the voice of the child, but it was first necessary to go out into the desert and, in poverty and thirst, discover in an experiential way that God sees everything. "Close your door, and your Father who sees in secret. . ." God sees everything; we know this in a very abstract way, but we must *discover it on the practical level.* Prayer opens us up to this discovery by revealing to us the marvelous transforming power of poverty, which passes from mere lack to dependence on the person we love. The fact that God knows our needs rescues us from our impoverished state, owing to the love that such a state makes clear.

And so, for us, prayer is no longer a teaching of God that is external to ús. In making us aware, little by little, of our real poverty, God gradually brings us to placing ourselves before him with trust, as beings who know they cannot do without him. Becoming conscious of our true desire, our true need, takes place *within* us; we have been brought to this light; we now understand it after so many roundabout efforts, which were, in a sense, stratagems of God's love for us. Since God already knows our needs, he looks forward to hearing them expressed again and again, not to burden or torment us but in order that by discovering their real dimension, we may realize their supreme value: *they are an opportunity to talk with him, as a son does with his Father.* One of the first spiritual masters, Evagrius, said that God delays in giving us what we need, perhaps first of all, because he enjoys hearing us speak to him. Of what importance are our needs . . . it is so good to stand before him and speak to him.

St. John Chrysostom remarked: "If God puts off
answering us, it is solely to keep us near him for
a longer time, as fathers do, who love their
children. 'But I am unworthy,' you say. Your
perseverance in prayer will make you worthy.
God often makes us wait in order to show himself more generous." Thus, the pedagogy of God
in prayer consists in drawing us more and more
to depend on him, and in this way helping us to
overcome the overwhelming discovery of our limitations by the certainty that this discovery leads
us to the secret of love.

GOD DOES NOT CHANGE

"God is not human,
that he should change his mind"

The Bible tells us of the extraordinary encounter
between God and Abraham that took place
before the destruction of Sodom and Gomorrah.
God had decided to annihilate Sodom, which will
actually be destroyed inspite of Abraham's supplication. In a magnificent instance of anthropo-
morphism, Genesis records the dialogue: "If there
be fifty just men in the city, will you then
destroy the place and not spare it for the sake of
the fifty just men? ... What if there be five less
than fifty just men? Will you destroy the whole
city on account of five? ... what if thirty be
found there?" (Genesis 18:23ff.). But God does
not change, and Sodom disappears amid the fire
and smoke.

"But We Do Not Know That We Wish It"

God does not change. We too come face to face
with the same immutability, we too discover one

day what Abraham experienced: that God would no longer be himself if he changed his mind, and that a God, given to human hesitation, would no longer be the one whom we await. "Every good gift and every perfect gift is from above, coming down from the Father of Lights, with whom there is no change, nor shadow of alteration" (James 1:17). But, then, why ask him to intervene? What's the use of telling him again and again of our misery, if the one to whom we cry cannot alter his wishes?

God does not change, and yet, "While God destroyed the cities of the region, he remembered Abraham and led Lot away from the catastrophe . . ." (Genesis 19:29). God saves Lot and his sons, but he does so in answer to Abraham's prayer. God's plans are unchangeable, but it would be distorting his providence to limit its influence solely to visible results, to apparent realities. Take the case, in our own day, of a foreman in a factory: he is responsible not only for the special problems of each piece of work that comes to him, but also for the order and unified effort of the whole operation. Likewise, the omnipotence of God is not restricted to deciding upon the existence of things; in the same act by which it makes things, it is involved in establishing the reason and order by which they will survive. *God is immutable in his designs, but the prayer of his children enters into these designs.* The purpose of prayer is not to change the order established by God, but to obtain what God has decided to accomplish by means of our prayer. *God wants the working out of certain things to depend on our desire and our prayer.* It pleases him that the prayer of those he loves should play a part in the realization of his designs.

We must be very clear on this point, and not imagine that the effectiveness of prayer depends on some kind of miracle. No, the process intended by God includes participation by us. If we should throw a match into a forest, we may start a fire, even though we are unaware of this or learn of it only later. The same is true of prayer. An awareness of ourselves, of our initiative and freedom, has nothing to do with miracles, but with an order of things presided over by love. We have been made to cooperate with our own destiny and the working out of history.

Fundamentally, we could reduce everything that happens in our life to two kinds of events:

1. that which happens to us, and over which we have no control;
2. that which we can obtain and achieve by our own effort and industry.

If we do not pray, we remain purely passive with regard to the events of the first category, while we attribute to our own efforts those of the second (including here a rather large margin of illusion). In prayer, we substitute God's will for our own. We enter into a plan which is that of God. We can situate ourselves on the wavelength of this project, and discover that God is our contemporary and that he "invents" our life with us. God wants us to take part in his work, a part so real that he presents himself to us as if he wanted to be conquered by our prayer. Without any exaggeration, it is really we who, in a certain sense, fulfill the desires of God. He does not want to do without us what he has decided to do with us.

Because of Abraham, Lot is saved, and Nineveh is spared because of the penance done by her sons. Denys the Syrian explains this as follows:

those who pray are like men in a boat who move the boat by pulling on the ropes attached to a certain spot on the shore. The rock to which the ropes are tied does not move, but the men bring the boat in by pulling on the rope lines. The sailors, however, do not move the buoy or the pier. Likewise, he who prays does not change God. Praying is pulling the bark of the Church toward God. And it is we, and not God, our will, our plans, that arrive on the shore. The greatest prayer we can make will be to say, like Christ: "Thy will be done." Not that his will should change, but that it will be accomplished; that it may be manifested in all its marvelous wisdom in order that we can unite ourselves to it and desire more and more precisely what God desires. Bernanos writes in *The Diary of a Country Priest*: "We really wish our death as He wishes it. We wish all that He wishes, *but we do not know that we wish it.* We do not know ourselves. Sin makes us live on the surface of ourselves; we enter within ourselves only to die and that is where He awaits us."

Thus, God does not change, but prayer is the means whereby he shares his plan with us. This is evident in the example of Abraham: at the moment of punishing him, God questions Abraham as if he were afraid to "surrender" himself: "Can I keep from Abraham what I am about to do?" (Genesis 18:17). God is reluctant to transmit his secrets, because in revealing them he would make of Abraham his friend; he would draw him into his plan through a feeling of love, and thereby submit himself, "bind" himself, to his desires. To Moses who invokes him after the making of the golden calf, God says, to liberate himself: "Let me alone, then, that my wrath may blaze up against them to consume them" (Exodus

32:10). And Catherine of Siena has God say: "I am caught by the chains of your desires; but those chains I myself forged." It was as if God aroused the desires of Abraham, Moses and his other friends in order to cover them over with his almighty power. In his eternal plan, God reserved a place for our prayer, and he does not change. This is the only source of the efficacy of prayer, and therefore of our hope. It is God himself who took the initiative of introducing Abraham into his plans and revealing his secrets to him: "Can I keep from Abraham what I am about to do?" And God does not hold back, for he loves Abraham.

This is one of the strangest and deepest aspects of prayer, and of the Christian mystery in general, which we can express in the words of St. Thomas: "Love did not permit God to remain alone." God is love, and love tends to share everything it has. God did not want to be alone in view of the happiness he could share and the world he could save. To us he wanted to be able to say, on the last day: "You had a part in the working out of it all."

In our prayer, do we realize, that we are speaking to God as the Almighty One, that is, he who controls the entire destiny of the universe and of each being in the universe? Are we conscious of the fact that, in prayer, the almighty power of God is, as it were, put at our disposal, with its universal power and its effect on the intimate life of each man? At certain moments, it seems as if God was abandoning everything to us. Isn't this one of the meanings of the image suggested in Scripture by the expression, "God is asleep" (cf. Psalms 77:65, 43:24; Isaiah 51:9; Psalm 93:1, and especially the scene in Mark 4:38).

God waits until the desire for his work springs forth in us. In St. John's view, becoming a disciple of Christ consists precisely in becoming capable of expressing within oneself, and addressing to the Father, Christ's own wishes: "I have called you friends, because all things that I have heard from my Father I have made known to you. ... I have chosen you, and have appointed you that you should go and bear fruit ... that whatever you ask the Father in my name he may give you. ... In this is my Father glorified, that you may bear very much fruit" (John 15:15-16). Although each man's efforts are obviously of a limited scope, is it not through our prayer and our desire that we share in the fullness of God's work and go beyond the limitations of our actions?

Would not awareness of this fact enlarge the special requests and prayers that we tend to confine to our own immediate, sometimes petty, concerns? Meditate upon the dimensions and realism that our prayer could have, and upon the bold, confident commitment that God's people would show if prayer were clearly understood as participation in the working out of God's plan.

"Before They Call. . ."

"Love did not permit God to remain alone," St. Thomas says again and again, to express the extraordinary and unique quality of Christianity. For the pre-Christians, Plato, the Stoics or Plotinus, man was only a *spectator* in the City of God. On the other hand, when St. Paul wishes to establish the role that can be ours, he explains it with one word: "We are God's *helpers*" (I Corinthians 3:9). And with Paul, all the saints have repeated this in their own words. For example,

St. Theresa of Lisieux says, in her *Letters*: "Why then did Jesus say: 'Ask the master of the harvest to send workers.' Isn't Jesus all-powerful? Oh, but Jesus has such an incomprehensible love for us that he wants us to have a part with him in the saving of souls; he wants to do nothing without us. The creator of the universe waits for the prayer of one poor, little soul to save other souls, who are redeemed like it at the price of his blood. These are the words of Jesus: 'Lift your eyes and see... See how in heaven there are empty places, and it is up to you to fill them. You are all Moses praying on the mountain. Ask me for workers, I will send some; I am only waiting for one prayer, one sigh from your heart.' If these were not the words of Jesus, who would dare believe them?"

Love did not allow God to remain alone. God, it is true, does not change, but in conformity with his plan, he is waiting to give us, in our prayer, an opportunity to fill the places he has set aside. And we enter into the New Testament when we understand that Christ wanted to be loved as a person and that he waits for our desire to participate in his plan and our joy in praying to him.

God knows everything. God does not change. Through prayer, we witness the utmost delicacy of a God who wished to do his work in response to his friends, even to the point of saying: "Before they call, I will answer" (Isaiah 65:24).

Doesn't the Bible contain examples wherein, despite the prayer made to him, God does not change his mind? See, among others: Genesis 18 (Abraham); II Samuel 12:15ff. (David); II Kings 20, and Isaiah 38 (Ezechia); and the episode of Jonas. Sometimes God does not want his answer to be as fast in coming as man would like. See Exodus 32,33 (Moses); the book of Job (*passim*): Samuel 12-18 (the entire history of David after the adultery and up to the death of Absalom).

When God delays his response, does he do so out of pleasure, or is it not rather to let us come to the point where he wants us to arrive? Read II Peter 3:9. Judith realized the mistake of accusing God of delay in manifesting himself; for this she makes the people do penance. Read Judith 8:10-27 (especially verses 15, 16, 17) and 9:5-6.

On the basis of the great prayers that the Bible has preserved for us, for example, those of Abraham, Moses, and, finally and above all, those of Christ, we can try to give a first definition of prayer. Prayer seems to us to be the *confrontation of two desires*: man's desire and the desire of God, or rather the *assumption of man's desire into that of God*. These two "desires" are present in every true prayer, and are sustained by mutual love. Prayer is an encounter made within the love of friendship; but this is a friendship initiated by God. As a result, this encounter brings about *the accommodation, the subordination, of the plans and desires of man with those of God*. "Let your will, not mine, be done" — "Let it be done unto me according to thy word" — "Thy will be done on earth as it is in heaven." These are the most perfect expressions of prayer, and the ultimate wish of genuine love.

READINGS

IT IS TO A GOD WE PRAY

A god to whom a person does not pray is

certainly not the true God. If we admit this, we realize, first, that if our idea of God does not encourage us to pray to him, this idea is not a true one. It also means accepting the fact that only those who pray have the right to talk to us about God. This is why we should consider below the statements of Christians who are speaking to God. Like them, we realize that one reaches God only through his help.

Praying to God means believing that he leads us on our way. But how does he lead us? From within. "Lead, kindly light," said Newman. Praying to God means believing that he is right. But how is he right? Through love.

YOU KNOW OUR SADNESS

Thou who hast first loved us, O God, alas! We speak of it in terms of history as if Thou hast only loved us first but a single time, rather than that without ceasing. Thou hast loved us first many times and everyday and our whole life through. When we wake up in the morning and turn our soul toward Thee — Thou art the first — Thou hast loved us first; if I rise at dawn and at the same second turn my soul toward Thee in prayer, Thou art there ahead of me, Thou hast loved me first. When I withdraw from the distraction of the day and turn my soul in thought toward Thee, Thou art the first and thus forever. And yet we always speak ungratefully as if Thou hast loved us first only once.

— Sören Kierkegaard, "Thou, Who Hast First Loved Us," in *The Prayers of*

Kierkegaard, ed, Perry D. LeFevre
(Chicago: University of Chicago Press,
1956), p. 14.

Lord our God, Thou knowest our sorrow
better than we know it ourselves. Thou
knowest how easily our fearful soul
entangles itself with untimely and self-
made cares. We pray Thee: Let us clearly
discern their inappropriateness and scorn
them proudly, these busy self-made cares.
But whatever care Thou dost inflict upon
us, let us receive it from Thy hand with
humility and give us the strength to bear
it.

> — Sören Kierkegaard, "Give Us The
> Strength," in *The Prayers of Kierke-
> gaard, op. cit.*, p. 72.

LEAD KINDLY LIGHT

Lead, Kindly Light, amid the encircling
                                        gloom,
   Lead Thou me on!
The night is dark, and I am far from home
   Lead Thou me on!
Keep Thou my feet; I do not ask to see
The distant scene, — one step enough
                                        for me.

I was not ever thus, nor prayed that Thou
   Shouldst lead me on;
I loved to choose and see my path,
                                        but now
   Lead Thou me on!
I loved the garish day, and, spite of fears,
Pride ruled my will: remember not
                                        past years.

So long Thy power hath blest me,
                              sure it still
    Will lead me on,
O'er moor and fen, o'er crag and torent,
                              till
    The night is gone;
And with the morn those angel faces
                              smile
Which I have loved long since,
                    and lost awhile.

> — John Henry Newman, *Lead Kindly
>   Light* (Boston: Roberts Brothers,
>   1884).

IT IS TO YOU I WANT TO GO

Now I love Thee alone.
... Order, I beg Thee, and command
what Thou wilt; but heal and open my
ears, so that with them I may hear Thy
words.
Heal and open my eyes so that with
them I may perceive Thy wishes.

Tell me where I should turn that I may
behold Thee; and I hope I shall do all
Thou hast commanded me.
Look, I beseech Thee, upon Thy
prodigal, O Lord, kindest Father.

Teach me how to come to Thee.
Nothing else do I have but willingness...
How I am to reach Thee I know not. Do
Thou inspire me, show me, give me what
I need for my journey.
If it is by faith that they find Thee
who have recourse to Thee, give me faith;

if it is through virtue, give me virtue; if it is by knowledge, give knowledge to me. Grant me increase of Faith, of Hope, and of Charity.

O how marvellous and extraordinary is Thy goodness.

To Thee do I appeal, and once more I beg of Thee the very means by which appeal is made to Thee... Grant that I may seek Thee, my Father; save me from error. When I seek Thee, let me not find aught else but Thee, I beseech Thee, Father. But if there is in me any vain desire, do Thou Thyself cleanse me and make me fit to look upon Thee.

... This only I shall ask of Thine extreme kindness, that Thou convertest me wholly to Thee, and that Thou allowest nothing to prevent me when I wend my way to Thee. Amen. Amen.

> — *The Soliloquies of Saint Augustine,*
> trans. Robert P. Russell (New York:
> Cosmopolitan Science and Art Service
> Co., Inc., 1943), pp. 13-14.

O God, Happiness, in Whom and by Whom and through Whom all those things are happy which are happy.

O God, Whom no one loses unless deceived, Whom no one seeks unless admonished, Whom no one finds unless he is purified.

O God, Whom to abandon is to perish, Whom to heed is to love, Whom to see is to possess.

O God, through Whom we overcome the enemy, Thee do I pray.

O God, through Whom we obtain that we do not altogether perish.

O God, by Whom we are admonished to be ever watchful.

O God, through Whom deprivations do not abase us.

O God, through Whom what is better in us is not under the dominion of our lower self.

O God, through Whom death is swallowed up in victory.

O God, Who dost convert us, stripping us of that which is not and clothing us with that which is.

O God, Who makest us worthy to be heard.

O God, Who strengthenest us; Who leadest us into all truth.

O God, Who speakest to us of all good things. . .

O God, Who callest us back to the way; Who leadest us to the gate; Who grantest that it its opened to them who knock.

O God, Who givest us the bread of life.

O God, through Whom we thirst for the cup, which when it is drunk we shall thirst no more.

O God, Who dost cleanse us, Who dost make us ready for divine rewards, graciously come to me.

> — *The Soliloquies of Saint Augustine*, *op. cit.*, pp. 7-9.

The purpose of prayer is perhaps less to obtain what we ask than to *become someone else*. We should go further and say that asking something

from God transforms us, little by little, into people
capable of sometimes doing without what they
ask for.

— Julien Green, *Journal*, III

In the true prayer relationship, it is not God
who hears what is asked of him, but he who
prays, and who continues to pray until he hears
what God wishes.

— Sören Kierkegaard, *Prières*, trans.
Tisseau (Bazoges-en-Pareds, 1957)

By faith he who is called Abraham obeyed by
going out into a place which he was to receive for
an inheritance; and he went out, not knowing
where he was going.

By faith he abode in the Land of Promise as in
a foreign land, dwelling in tents with Isaac and
Jacob, the co-heirs of the same promise.

For he was looking for the city with fixed
foundations, of which city the architect and
builder is God.

— Epistle to the Hebrews 11:8-10.

YOU ARE UNIQUE ...
YOU ARE ALSO MY BROTHER

Gentle Lord, Thou canst offer Thyself with such
love and tenderness that all hearts should desire
Thee, and have an ardent longing for Thy love.
The words of love flow so full of life from Thy
sweet mouth that they have wounded many
hearts in the flower of their youth so deeply that
all transient love was completely extinguished in
them. Ah, gentle Lord, my heart longs, my mind
yearns; I should gladly hear Thee speak of it.

Speak, then, my only chosen comfort, one little word to my soul, Thy poor handmaid, for under Thy shadow I have sweetly fallen asleep, but my heart is wakeful.

> — Henry Suso, *Little Book of Eternal Wisdom and Little Book of Truth,* trans. James M. Clark (New York: Harper, 1953), p. 71.

. . . Beloved Lord, if my heart had the love of all hearts, if my conscience had the clarity of all angels, and my soul the beauty of all souls, if I were worthy of it by Thy grace, Lord, then would I fain receive Thee today as lovingly and submerge Thee into the depths of my heart and my soul, so that neither life nor death would ever divide me from Thee.

. . . Sweet, fair Lord . . . for Thou art the only One in Whom all things are included that my heart can desire in time or eternity. . . Thou art indeed the very fairest to the eyes. . . Thy presence inflames me, but Thy majesty terrifies me. My reason wishes to honor its Lord, but my heart wishes to love, and affectionately embrace its only love, and, if I dare say it, my beloved Spouse. Ah, what love, what bliss, what joy, what honor I have in Thee alone!

> — Henry Suso, *Little Book of Eternal Wisdom and Little Book of Truth, op. cit.,* pp. 140-41.

HE PUTS HIMSELF AT OUR MERCY

He makes himself poor in order that we might offer him our charity; he puts forth his hand to us like a *beggar* in order that on the bright day of judgment, when he shall appear in his glory, we may hear these sweet words: "Come, blessed of my Father for I was hungry and you gave me to eat; I was thirsty and you gave me to drink; I was a stranger and you took me in. . . I was in prison and you came to me."

It is Jesus himself who pronounced these words, it is he who wishes our love, who *begs* for it. . . He puts himself, as it were, at our mercy. He wants to take nothing unless we give it to him, and the smallest thing is precious in his divine sight.

> — St. Theresa of the Child Jesus, *Letter 124, to Céline*

PARADISE OF HAPPINESS, UNAPPROACHABLE LIGHT

You are holy, Lord, God Almighty,
Father of our Lord Jesus Christ,
Paradise of happiness, royal scepter,
    sumptuous love, certain hope, faith.
You are holy, Lord God,
You are the King of kings and Lord
    of lords,
Only you possess immortality;
You live in an unapproachable light,
    which no one has ever seen.
You sit with the Cherubims and Thrones,
You walk o'er the winds,
You created heaven, earth, sea and
    all they enclose. . .
You made the winds your messengers
    and burning fire your servant,
You made man in your image and
    likeness,

You measured the heavens with your
hand and all the earth with your
finger;
Yes, your works are very beautiful,
in your presence.

— Prayer of the Early Christians

In his sight we set our hearts at rest. Because if
our heart blames us, God is greater than our
heart. . .

— First Epistle of St. John 3:10-20

HOW CAN YOU LEAVE ME?

Where are your feet so that you might henceforth
flee from me, and how will you go about it?

To whom will you extend your hands, I ask
you, now that I have taken away your sight?

Where is the river bank that you did not
exhaust? What adventure remains for you, and
what love?

It was exactly the time for me to make you
blind and deaf!

Am I really your God? Did you think you
could get away from me so easily?

And despite everything I have done to you, is
it so easy not to love me?

It was hard to cruelly forbid you the things I
gave you, simply because I was not there,

This meal which from the first taste disgusted
you, because I was far away.

But what do you think of this banquet now,
which we eat in solitude and intimacy?

Where I am, is the eternal secret of your birth.

You struggle in vain, you will not defend yourself forever against my peace.

Do you, or do you not, sense that I am there, this guest whom you were waiting for?

Is the rest I offer deep enough for you? What do you say, poor heart?

Unless we were different, there would not be this desire, there would not be this embrace as between spouses!

If you were not my son, today I would not be the Father around whose neck the prodigal son throws his arms.

Since we have finally reached each other in abdication and effort.

To avoid preferring me, it would be necessary that you not know me.

He whom I admit even unto my own being, how will he die?

Where are your hands, which are not mine? And your feet, which are not fastened to the same cross? Where are you, you who do not listen to me?

How can you leave me without tearing out my heart?

— Paul Claudel, *La messa là-bas*

Because you are precious in my eyes and glorious, and because I love you, I give men in return for you and peoples in exchange for your life.

— Isaiah 43:4.

EVERYTHING YOU WISH

No! I could have no other will but yours, my Lord! I gave you my will once, and I will never take it back; it is forever lost and submerged in yours. May everything you wish be done, every-

thing you wish take place, whatever it may be. . .
May your will be done, my God . . . I know that
your will is your glory, your treasure. . . May it
be done. . . Oh, God, grant that I and all those
over whom you have given me special charge, all
the faithful of your Church, all men, may do
your will. Amen! Amen!

> — Charles de Foucauld, *Ecrits Spirituals*
> (De Gigord, 1927), p. 166.

O my Lord, how true a Friend Thou art, and
how powerful! For Thou canst do all Thou wilt
and never dost Thou cease to will if we love
Thee. Let all things praise Thee, Lord of the
world. Oh, if someone would but proclaim
throughout the world how faithful Thou art to
Thy friends! All things fail, but Thou, Lord of
them all, failest never. Little is the suffering that
Thou dost allow to those who love Thee. O my
Lord, how delicately and skillfully and delectably
canst Thou deal with them! Oh, would that we
had never stayed to love anyone save Thee!
Thou seemest, Lord, to give severe tests to those
who love Thee, but only that in the extremity of
their trials they may learn the greater extremity
of Thy love.

> — *The Life of the Holy Mother Teresa
> of Jesus*, in *The Complete Works of
> Saint Teresa of Jesus*, trans. E. Allison
> Peers (New York: Sheed and Ward,
> 1957), vol. I, p. 163.

May His Majesty help me to find comfort in
what is really comfort, to call honour what is
really honour and to take delight in what is really
delight — and not the other way round. Not a fig
shall I care then for all the devils in hell: it is
they who will fear me.

— *The Life of the Holy Mother Teresa
of Jesus, op. cit.*, p. 165.

Do not be satisfied with what you understand
about God, nourish yourself instead on what you
do not understand about him. Do not base your
happiness and delight on what you may hear or
feel of him, but rather on what you can neither
feel nor hear. . . God is always hidden; continue
to serve him as he is thus hidden in secret, even
when you may think you have found, felt and
heard him. The less one understands, the closer
one gets to him.

— St. John of the Cross

THANK THE LORD

As the hind longs for the running waters, so my
soul longs for you, O God. Athirst is my soul for
God, the living God. When shall I go and behold
the face of God? My tears are my food day and
night, as they say to me day after day, "Where is
your God?" Those times I recall, now that I
pour out my soul within me, when I went with
the throng and led them in procession to the
house of God, amid loud cries of joy and thanksgiving, with the multitude keeping festival. Why
are you so downcast, O my soul? Why do you
sigh within me? Hope in God! For I shall again
be thanking him, in the presence of my savior
and my God.

Within me my soul is downcast; so will I
remember you from the land of the Jordan and
of Hermon, from Mount Misar. Deep calls unto
deep in the roar of your cataracts; all your
breakers and your billows pass over me. By day
the Lord bestows his grace, and at night I have

his song, a prayer to my living God. I sing to
God, my Rock: "Why do you forget me? Why
must I go about in mourning, with the enemy
oppressing me?" It crushes my bones that my
foes mock me, as they say to me day after day,
"Where is your God?" Why are you so downcast,
O my soul? Why do you sigh within me? Hope
in God! For I shall again be thanking him, in the
presence of my savior and my God.

— Psalm 41

My God, if I did not exist,
You would not exist either,
Since I am you,
With that need that you have of me.

— Angelius Silesius

II

HOW TO PRAY

"We do not know what we should pray for as we ought, but the Spirit helps our weakness."

— ROMANS 8:26

"The Spirit himself intercedes. . ."

THE GREAT LAWS OF PRAYER

ONE of the first observations to be made about our prayer life is that we do not know how to pray. The Apostles themselves recognized this very soon and make this request to Christ: "And it came to pass as he was praying in a certain place, that when he ceased, one of his disciples said to him, 'Lord, teach us how to pray, even as John also taught his disciples'" (Luke 11:1). Like them, we too discover the necessity of learning how to pray. "I don't know how to pray." To admit this is a sign that we are truthful, and it prompts us to find out whether there are any "rules" of prayer, or else a procedure, a liturgical method, or some other method (cf. the success of yoga and other techniques of prayer).

It seems to us that one of the first qualities of prayer is its *spontaneity*. In prayer, we want to express the true part of ourselves, freely. And we are justifiably unimpressed by stereotyped formulas which prevent us from finding the best part of ourselves. Can we, then, speak of "laws" in prayer without introducing something artificial and non-authentic? Do we have to falsify our personality even before God? Must we play a role, as we do before men, in order to obey certain rules of prayer?

But just as someone's love is never acquired once and for all, so prayer is never a formula that can be pronounced once and for all time. Perhaps this is why Christ hardly ever heeded a request as quickly as this one, "Teach us how to pray." If prayer is a discussion, a conversation with God, we must first learn to speak the language of God in our heart and soul: "For who among men knows the things of a man save the spirit of the man which is in him? Even so, the things of God no one knows but the Spirit of God" (I Corinthians 2:11). "No one can say 'Jesus is Lord,' except in the Holy Spirit" (I Corinthians 12:3). "But in like manner the Spirit also helps our weakness. For we do not know what we should pray for as we ought, but the Spirit himself pleads for us with unutterable groanings" (Romans 8:26). The first step in every prayer, therefore, is to ask Christ, the Spirit, once again to teach us how to pray. We will now, then, examine the great parables in which Christ stated his own thoughts on prayer, in order to discover its essential laws.

FIRST LAW: LIKE A POOR MAN

The Parable of the Pharisee and the Publican (Luke 18:9-14). One of the first difficulties in prayer is to know whether we should be concerned with formulas; whether, at the moment of our prayer, we should strive to specify exactly what we mean; or, more simply, whether the essential point is not, above and beyond the formulas and requests, the *attitude* we should assume. In the above parable, our Lord answers these questions by showing us that the essential point in our prayer is to learn how to present ourselves *as poor men*.

The Three Reasons: St. John of the Cross has indicated, in a marvelous way, the reasons why we should give preference to attitude rather than to formulas: "The reason why it is better for the person who loves to express his needs to the beloved, rather than ask him to satisfy such needs, arises from three factors: first, because our Lord knows better than we what is proper for us; secondly, because the loved one has more compassion in seeing the need of the one who loves and is more impressed by his feeling of resignation; thirdly, because a person is less given to self-love and formality when expressing what he is lacking than in asking for what he only seems to need."

This is confirmed rather consistently in all the examples of Scripture: neither the Virgin nor the followers of Christ made particular requests, but only expressed their needs to Christ. What does the Virgin say at Cana? Not "Could you give them wine?" but "they have no wine" (John 2:3). What do the sisters of Lazarus say at the time of his death? "Lord, behold, he whom thou lovest is sick" (John 11:3). Likewise the centurion at Capharnaum (Matthew 8:6), and the Chanaanite woman (Matthew 15:22-28).

This is also the lesson of the Old Testament. Note how the mother of Samuel presents herself: "I am only a poor woman" (I Samuel 1:15).

But the most significant example seems to be the entire history of Moses. It is not his great feats that bring about the deliverance of the people, nor his assurance or his eloquence before Pharoah. On the contrary, all these human efforts have only one, single result: Pharoah hardens his stand and each time refuses to let the Jews go (cf. Exodus, chaps. 7-10). It is in his weakness that Moses, greatly discouraged, at last expresses his real prayer (cf. Exodus 3:11 "Who am I? . . ."; Exodus 4:10-5:21-23). He will later express himself freely before God, in giving vent to the exhaustion inflicted on him by the demands of the people (Numbers 11:4: "I cannot carry all this people by myself, for they are too heavy for me. If this is the way you will deal with me, then please do me the favor of killing me at once. . ."). Moses explains the impossibility and fatigue that his mission presents, in view of the fact that he is the victim of the Pharoah's sarcasm and irony, and the people's lack of faith and protestations. He is afraid; *but in his fear and his weakness, he learns how to talk to God.* Likewise, Elias, a victim of discouragement, asks to die (I Kings 19:4-5). Jeremias, too, at the moment of his call (Jeremias 1:6), and especially in the great exhaustion stemming from his mission, expresses discouragement (Jeremias 20:7-13). Finally, and above all, we have the example set by Christ at Gethsemane (Matthew 26:36).

When God intervenes, we can no longer mistake the fact that he alone can assist us. Yahweh responds to Moses with the answer he will give to everyone: "I will be with you" (Exodus 3:12; see also Jeremias 1). Likewise, the response of the Angel to Mary (Luke 1:28). Also, the prayer of Christ at the moment of excruciating suffering, which prompts him to ask for deliverance from his appointed hour (John 12:27). In the Garden of Olives, an angel is sent to fortify him (Luke

22:43). God intervenes when a person can no longer be mistaken (Exodus 10:1-2—17:3-6).

All this is contained in the Parable of the Pharisee and the Publican, where our Lord shows us that God does not resist the attitude of the poor person. "But the publican, standing afar off, would not so much as lift up his eyes to heaven, but kept striking his breast, saying, 'O God, be merciful to me the sinner! ' I tell you, this man went back to his home justified rather than the other. . ." (Luke 18:13-14).

Is it not normal that the experience of poverty should provoke an attitude of discontent — which is not prayer — which the Bible calls the "murmurings" of the people? The people complain to Yahweh, in the person of Moses, for having brought them to their desperate position: "Would that we had died in the land of Egypt, or that here in the desert we were dead! Why is the Lord bringing us into this land only to have us fall by the sword? " (Numbers 14:2-4). Likewise, when the Jews confront our Lord (John 6:41-43), and also the Apostles themselves (John 6:60).

Is it not normal for man to try to assert his independence, his autonomy? Does not accepting poverty mean accepting a conversion, agreeing to change the fundamental direction of one's life? Thereafter, we depend on someone else. The serious factor in refusing one's impoverished state, is the refusal to live under the guidance, and in the dependence, of someone else. This is the attitude of the people in the desert: they refuse to live by relying on God, and, what is more, they demand that he account for what has happened to them. This is also the position of the Pharisees toward Christ. And what about ourselves? Do we accept this state of dependence, and more importantly, do we know how to find in it one of the secrets of our existence? Can we recognize in it the true source of peace and joy in love? In examining our religious life and our success in prayer, should we not first of all question ourselves as to whether we accept or refuse this state of dependence on God and on Christ?

By accepting and even willing our poverty, we do not rejoice in our state of need, but rejoice in the fact that *it is an opportunity to depend on someone else.* This is one of the meanings of the verb, "to believe," in the Bible: "to let oneself be carried along by another." On the other hand, if evangelical poverty were only a lack, only the absence of something we need, should we not justifiably avoid it?

All this does not mean that in actually working out our life of prayer, there will not be formulas. Actually, prayer always contains one, at least in outline. We must recall, however, that the formulation of this is not necessarily expressed in words or distinct intellectual concepts. At the minimum, prayer can consist of but a cry from the heart, a glance toward God. But this should by no means induce us to laziness. On the contrary, when our disinterest is certain, we should often try to make specific requests, such as in matters that pertain, for example, to the Church: that it should live according to the Beatitudes, accept poverty, not be concerned with temporal results, maintain the courage that is born of prayer, etc.

In conclusion, this first law of prayer suggests that *prayer is something very simple.* We have no right to say that conversation with God is difficult, complicated. Our first concern should not be to seek out formulas or find out what would be best for us to obtain, but rather to *learn how to talk to God, in our state of weakness.* This is the first secret, the first law, of prayer (cf. the great charter of poverty, as St. Paul expressed it: II Corinthians 11:16 to 12:10, especially 12:5,9,10).

We should not be surprised if God begins his teaching process by unveiling all our illusions, in order to bring us to the truth. In fact, if he does love us, God cannot allow us to be in error regarding our true happiness. Accepting someone's love, means also allowing him to feel jealous over us — the jealousy of truth. We would not want a love that would allow us to remain in a state of illusion. Moreover, through the discovery of our impoverished state, God leads us to purifying our desire and makes of us *men in waiting.* "Take heed, watch and pray" (Matthew 24:42-44 and 26:40-43; Mark 13:33; Luke 21:34-36). Note, in this connection, the pedagogy of God with regard to *all* the saints: Moses (Exodus 3:11-12, etc.), St. Paul (II Corinthians 12:5), St. Francis of Assisi (who dies practically an exile from his Order, poor, even because of what he did for God), Charles de Foucauld (who dies abandoned by those very people to whom he devoted himself). In each case, God seems to bring those who love him to *prefer him above everything else.* Our prayer is true only when, as a result of it, we choose God once again, only if it gives evidence that we prefer him over all the "idols" that are put before us — money, friends, various talents, etc. — but which are not, in a word, God. Then is our prayer truly a response to the call of a God who loves us.

Can it be said that God takes pleasure in seeing

us poor? Is not the discovery of our poverty, first
of all, a means of showing forth God's opulence?
Does not sharing it with us attach us to it? In
the case of Moses and the saints, does not the
experience of setbacks have a meaning that is
beyond them? The reticence of Pharaoh (which
impressed on Moses his own powerlessness),
brought to a state of paroxysm, was perhaps
necessary so that the liberation of the people
might appear to everyone as the work of God
alone. *The departure from Egypt had to be a
work of love in order to make clear to the people
what their God was really like* (read Osee 11,
especially verses 3,4: "Yet it was I who taught
Ephraim to walk, who took them in my arms. I
drew them with human cords, with hands of love;
I fostered them like one who raises an infant to
his cheeks; yet, though I stooped to feed my
child, they did not know that I was their
healer"). So that the people might remember God
as God of love, was it not necessary that they
have an absolute experience of it and learn to
depend on God alone, and thereby experience at
the same time their own powerlessness and
impoverishment?

Likewise, in our own life, God can reveal his
concern for us only if, at certain moments, we
realize that he alone can free us, and only if, on
certain days, we place our trust in him — and in
him alone. This is the real meaning we can attach
to Gandhi's expression: "Prayer is the daily
admission of one's weakness." and more pro-
foundly to St. Paul's statement, "When I am
weak, then I am strong" (read 11 Corinthians
12:9-10).

*Is not the authenticity of our prayer measured,
in large part, by the attitude we have regarding*

our state of weakness? Do we ever examine ourselves on this point?

SECOND LAW: "IN ALL CIRCUMSTANCES DO NOT LOSE HEART"

In the parable of those invited to the banquet, the Gospel shows us God looking for worshippers, for those whom he could invite to dialogue and friendship with him. It also shows us that he foresaw the reasons why people decline the invitation (Luke 14:16-24): "And they all with one accord began to excuse themselves. The first said to him, 'I have bought a farm, and I must go out and see it; I pray thee hold me excused.' And another said, 'I have bought five yoke of oxen, and I am on my way to try them. . .' And another said, 'I have married a wife, and therefore I cannot come.' " All these reasons can be reduced to two: concern for one's family, and the necessity of earning a living. If, then, consideration of one's family and earning a living are sufficient reasons for declining God's invitation to pray, who will actually be able to pray? If prayer is reserved for those who have no family or who do not work, what people are intended here? And can we say that the problem, "I don't have the time," is a valid one?

The parable leads us to conclude that *everyone is summoned* and that we are not justified in arguing that work and fatigue are obstacles to a life of prayer. This is not to deny that the effort required in prayer is difficult. But the difficulty here is normal: as much as we would like to, on the human level, we cannot "feel" the mystery of God, otherwise he would no longer be God. The best witnesses to the difficulty of prayer are the

Apostles themselves: after a few years of living together with Christ, they still were not capable of spending one hour of prayer with him, for example, at the time of his Agony (Mark 14:37). The great temptation will be fatigue, and all the best of reasons will be put forward to excuse us, to serve as an alibi. Our Lord puts special emphasis on this question: of the three parables on prayer, two are stated in very forceful terms. It seems that the great obstacle to our prayer, in Christ's eyes, was discouragement, fatigue.

"Wear Me Out"

Our Lord responds to this problem with two parables in which he shows the importance of perseverance: the parable of the importunate friend (Luke 11:5-13), and that of the widow and the unjust judge (Luke 18:1-8). In both parables, our Lord uses the technique of contrast: if we admit that a human judge, cynically egotistic, can reward the perseverance of someone who means nothing to him, how can we doubt that God, who is infinitely good, will not reward the perseverance of his children? Likewise, in the parable of the importunate friend: the grumpy man who is asleep in no sense represents God; but if we admit that egotism will yield to insistent demands, how much more the goodness of the Father "who will not give a stone, a serpent or a scorpion, when one of you asks for a loaf of bread, a fish or an egg."

Note the forcefulness of the terms chosen by our Lord; three of them have special significance: "And he also told them a parable — that they must *always (in all circumstances) pray and not lose heart*" (Luke 18:1). Next, "Because this widow bothers me, I will do her justice, lest *by her continual coming she finally wear me out"* (Luke 18:5). And finally, "And will not God avenge his elect, who cry to him *day and night"* (Luke 18:7). The parable is very explicit: day and night, we must appear before God like men determined to "wear him out," until his Kingdom arrives. Note, however, that the Greek expression used by the evangelist leads us not to take the work "continually" in a purely material sense; it is better understood as meaning "in all circumstances." Thus, we are reminded once again of the necessity of taking time out to pray.

We should, then, emphasize that the first two laws of prayer are related to one another: if a poor man is really poor, he does not cease trying to obtain what he needs. If, therefore, the first law consists essentially of recognizing our poverty, our need of God, and if this need is real, it is only natural that the second law should emphasize the necessity of expressing this need *unceasingly*, until it is satisfied, that is until the Kingdom of God appears.

In a single question we can summarize all those questions that are asked regarding the above: *Is it not better to pray little and well, instead of a great deal?* In answer, we should restate the question in two ways:

1. *Do we have the right to pray little?*

Let us consider:
— *the massive testimony of the early Church* in the Acts of the Apostles (the passages referred to constitute, as it were, laws for the entire history of the Church). Let us find again the exact words

used ("continually" — "they did not cease to
pray," etc. See Acts 1:14, 10:2, 12:5, 16:25,
20:7).

— *the teaching of our Lord* (Luke 11:5-13,
18:1-8; Matthew 7:7-11).

— *the teaching of St. Paul and St. Peter*
(Romans 12:12; Philippians 4:6; Ephesians 5:20;
Colossians 4:2, II Peter 3:9).

— *the testimony of those to whom God
revealed himself* (Luke 2:37: the elderly Anna,
etc. On the contrary, see the harsh reaction of
God when the children of Israel forget him, while
he himself is waiting for them, in Judges 3:7-9).

— *the testimony of the prophets:* the extraordinary parable of the watchman, and the fate
assigned to him by Scripture if he lets himself fall
asleep (Isaiah 62:6-7; Ezechiel 33:1-20).

— lastly, *the very example of our Lord:* "But I
am not alone, because the Father is with me"
(John 16:32); "He continued all night in prayer
to God" (Luke 6:12).

2. *Do we know when we pray well?*

— Read again Luke 18:9-14, and also Luke
16:15: "You are they who declare yourselves just
in the sight of men" [you assume that you pray
well] .

Quantity or quality, which of the two should
prevail in our prayer? Scripture gives us the
answer: we must not measure the time, God
waits for everything. God is always waiting for
us, and in his eyes there are no such things as
interruptions. On the other hand, we are never
sure of what is really quality.

"It Is Our Heart God Listens To"

All The Time. The real solution here suggests that we should not have any illusions about the application of our effort. To pray "continually," would be impossible, if prayer, for us, meant a purely intellectual meditation. Similarly, "if prayer depended on the body, we could not pray and be occupied manually at the same time; if it were a matter of sensibility, every sensible preoccupation, sickness, emotion, would make it impossible, and it would be subject to our change of moods; if it were solely in the brain, we would pray only when we would be discussing theology. But prayer is, above all, within our selves: our 'heart' can always pray to God; even when our hands are busy, our sensibility crushed and our head burdened with worries, it can always talk about what makes its life and its love most meaningful. On the contrary, when our 'heart' is concerned about something other than God, prayer then ceases within us. It is actually our 'heart' that God listens to" (B.-M. Chevignard, O.P.).

The important thing to note, therefore, is that it is by our will and our heart that we are united to God. Then we can understand where continual prayer resides: in the direction in which our will moves, in the most basic desire of our heart. As to actual deeds, in this life it is not possible to be always in the *actual process* of prayer; but the movement of one's love is a dynamic reality which continues to exist, even if one is scarcely conscious of it.

Modern-day psychology teaches us to what extent we are under the permanent influence of our deepest tendencies, even when we do not realize it. The purpose of prayer should be to liberate, little by little, the tendency within us to converse with God at every moment, to transform every event and every circumstance into an occasion for opening ourselves to God and recalling his presence.

This leads us to distinguishing between the act of prayer and the state of prayer, and to realizing that we must look far beyond the simple "act." We should not restrict the perseverance to which our Lord summons us in his parables, to a question of milieu or of one's daily schedule. We should not complain of the external obstacles to our life of prayer, the furious pace of life that surrounds us, for it is *within us* that we must learn to become, little by little, independent of all this. Similarly, the fidelity on which our Lord puts such emphasis is, above all, an internal fidelity of the deepest part of our will.

"No Matter What It May Cost"

Some Time. The apprenticeship required for such interior fidelity and perseverance can succeed only if we decide to devote a certain amount of time each day to prayer. *To give all his time, a person need only give some of his time.* But this will be impossible if we pray only when we feel like praying. There is a certain illusion here: very soon we will no longer feel like opening ourselves to this dialogue which takes place in the context of faith. Very soon we will run the risk of allowing the ship to go adrift, and gradually fall victim to the intoxication of forgetfulness. Therefore, a certain amount of time is needed before a state of calm may enter the soul, before we can "recompose a certain interior order." It was not without intention that God insisted on periods of rest in the life of his people (Exodus 31:13-14, and 20:8-11). The law of the Sabbath, of a state of restfulness in prayer, was extremely important and sacred. Thus, we will not establish in ourselves, in a really stable way, the most important part of prayer — the tendency of the heart — unless we absolutely respect the rhythms of prayer: daily rhythm (the minimum would be fifteen minutes); weekly rhythm (for example, some time on Saturday to prepare for the next day's Mass, or even on Sunday itself); a longer time — a monthly rhythm (such as an afternoon or an entire day "dedicated" in a special way).

Many of our essential attitudes can arise in our life only if they come from inside of us: concern for our fellowmen, understanding of misery, care in the search for happiness, a true sense of the Redemption, consideration, based on faith, of weakness and mercy... All this is, to a great extent, the result of our fidelity or our lack of fidelity to our "times" for prayer.

"We don't have the time." Are we really consistent regarding this false pretext? Time seems very valuable to us when it is a matter of giving some to God, for such time strikes us as being very long. But can we say that we do not waste time very often? Do we not show great imagination when we sometimes try to "kill time"? Are we completely aware of our actual day-to-day "schedule"? And sufficiently aware of the serious Christian concern over the use of a person's time? Through circumstances more or less important, everything can become right, in our modern-day culture, for turning us away from consciousness of ourselves and of God.

We claim that prayer is a difficult thing. Should we not find fault more often with our own lack of courage? Did not Christ, and after

him the saints, warn us about this? It is true,
what is needed here is courage, and even a certain
kind of heroism, to be "faithful."

"How does a person begin to pray? I repeat:
what is important, is to have a firm resolution, an
absolute, unshakable determination, not to stop
until one reaches the fountainhead, no matter
what may happen or may enter into our lives,
and no matter what it may cost us" (St. Theresa,
Way of Perfection, Chap. 21).

But are we aware that the very act of praying
is already a form of grace, and one which must
be asked for, again and again?

Should we not also admit that it is not time
but faith which is lacking to us? Insofar as we
are convinced of the importance of prayer, we
will find ways to make room for it in our lives. If
it is only a luxury or a useless form of chatter,
there will surely be no time for it. But if it is a
necessity of life, as eating or sleeping are, then
the objection, "we don't have time," is absurd, as
absurd as that of a sick person saying to the
doctor that he does not have time to eat or take
his medicine; or as detestable as saying to one's
beloved that one does not have the time to think
of her.

In short, if sometimes we hardly know what
we should ask of God, one thing at least is
always in our power: perseverance, insistence. We
do not have the right to propose our life of daily
work and fatigue as an obstacle to the life of
prayer. We do not have the right to believe that
only moments of "retreat" are important, and
that outside of those we can exist on energy
previously stored up. We must understand that
every circumstance can become an "opportunity"
for talking with God. In view of what is
entrusted to us, we are not like "piece workers."

but instead like workers who are paid by the hour. It is not by the amount of work we do that God will judge us, but by the way in which we shall use the time given to us. It is the moment at hand that counts. *May my will at that time be directed toward God!*

THIRD LAW: "IN THE NAME OF JESUS"

Our Lord did not promise efficaciousness to every kind of prayer, but to that prayer which would be done in his name. Under this essential condition, the promise he made was a solemn one.

Evidence for this fact is repeated again and again in Scripture:

— John 14:13: "And whatever you *ask in my name*, that I will do, in order that the Father may be glorified in the Son."

— John 16:23-24: "Amen, amen, I say to you, if you ask the Father anything in my name, he will give it to you. Hitherto you *have not asked anything in my name.* Ask, and you shall receive, that your joy may be full."

— John 11:41-42: "Father, I give thee thanks that thou hast heard me. Yet I know that thou *always hearest me.*"

— St. John repeats this in a different way in his First Epistle (2:1): "But if anyone sins, we have an *advocate with the Father*, Jesus Christ the judge."

— Similarly St. Paul, Romans 8:33-34: "Who shall make accusation against the elect of God? It is God who justifies! Who shall condemn? It is Christ Jesus who died; yes, and rose again, *he who is at the right hand of God, who also intercedes for us.*"

— Hebrews 7:25: "Therefore he is able at all times to save those who come to God through him, since *he lives always to make intercession for them.*"

— Colossians 3:16-17: "Whatever you do in word or in work, *do all in the name of the Lord Jesus*, giving thanks to God the Father through him."

— Ephesians 3:11-12: ". . . according to the eternal purpose he accomplished in Christ Jesus our Lord. In him we have *assurance and confident access through faith in him.*"

— II Corinthians 1:20: "For all the promises of God find their 'Yes' in him; and *therefore through him also arises the 'Amen' to God unto our glory.*"

— Hebrews 9:14: ". . . how much more will the *blood of Christ*, who through the Holy Spirit offered himself unblemished unto God, cleanse your conscience from dead works to serve the living God?" And 13:15: "Through him, therefore, let us offer up a sacrifice of praise always to God. . ."

All these passages suggest an extremely important question that we should consider with regard to prayer: Do we really care about uniting ourselves to the desires of Christ? Are we concerned, first of all, with the thought Christ has for us, for each of "our activities"? Or is our prayer too often just the running of a kind of "interior film," intended just for ourselves? Or else a more or less melancholy, sterile monologue? Or a search for "ideas on" things, instead of being a profound examination of our soul for the purpose of listening to the real desires of Christ's soul and praying "in his name"?

In the Scriptural passages just cited, Christ

appears as the one whom the Epistle to the Hebrews calls our "High Priest," the one who never ceases to invoke his Father on behalf of mankind. St. John calls him "our advocate." What does this mean, if not that in heaven Christ is the one who presents to the Father our praise and adoration, as well as our requests. We could say that *he repeats our words before God, that he takes our feeble human language, transforms it and makes it his own.* This is the reason why our prayer is efficacious: because it becomes the prayer of Christ.

This is possible because it was Christ himself who left us the legacy of prayer. In this sense, Christian prayer is something *new*; it is a gift of Christ (Luke 11:1). It is *his prayer* that he gives us. Charity is a "new" commandment since, before the coming of Christ, we could not love as he does, with his spirit and even with his love. Thus, our Lord could say: "*Hitherto* you have not asked anything in my name. Ask, and you shall receive. . ." (John 16:24). Thereafter, prayer would be Christian only if it was identical with that of Christ, and if he himself would extend it to all the needs of the Kingdom, to the redemption of men of all times and places. Only in this way could it be "catholic," that is, total; otherwise, our prayer would remain a prayer of the Old Testament, which puts the mediation of Christ, the Incarnation and the Cross, as it were, "off to the side."

Prayer in His Name. Following the example of St. Augustine, we can explain how all this is possible by distinguishing three great aspects of this prayer made in the name of Christ: our Lord is the one *by* whom and *in* whom we give glory to the Father, and also *the one whom* we celebrate.

Christ is the one *by* whom we glorify the
Father: actually by ourselves we cannot really lay
claim to celebrating the Father, for we do not
know him. "No one knows the Father except the
Son, and him to whom the Son chooses to reveal
him" (Matthew 11:27). ". . . The things of God
no one knows but the Spirit of God. Now we
have received not the spirit of the world, but the
spirit that is from God, that we may know the
things that have been given us by God" (I Corinthians 2:11-12). Only our Lord can render true
worship, and he alone can offer it perfectly. He
is, so to speak, the "prototype" of the way in
which a sinful creature should conduct himself
before God. Thus, St. Paul remarks: "For all the
promises of God find their 'Yes' in him; and
therefore through him also rises the 'Amen' to
God unto our glory" (II Corinthians 1:20). There
is, as we know, only one face to which God
cannot remain unsensitive, that is, the face of his
Son.

Our Lord is the one "*in* whom we render all
honor and all glory to God"; the one in whom
we pray. The duty of the Church is to take up
the prayer of Christ to which we incorporate
ourselves. This means adopting the admiration,
joy and will of Christ with respect to his Father,
the submission to his plans, the passion for his
Kingdom. But all this is repeated by us as if it
were *we* who were so inspired, as if it all came
from *us*. We, in other words, do his work.
Accordingly, the liturgy consists in continuing
not only the presence but also the life of Christ.
The Church is composed of those people who are
chosen to live out those aspects of the redemp-
tive mystery which the glorious Christ no longer
lives out. This is what St. Paul means when he
states: "Have this mind in you which was also in

Christ Jesus" (Philippians 2:5). When we pray, we actualize a reality which exists in us since baptism; we activate a form of energy that is antecedent to our prayer: the presence in us of the Spirit of Christ by means of sanctifying grace. To a certain extent, all we are then doing is recognizing the reality that exists within us and that is allowed to express itself by "the Spirit who lives in our hearts." Being "in prayer," involves, therefore, a conscious effort to enter *into* the mystery of Christ. We must learn to address ourselves to God only *in* Christ. This constitutes the reality of "Christian" prayer. We must develop more and more the consciousness of recognizing and glorifying in Christ "Our Father," that is, his Father and also our Father. We are beings inhabited by Christ; we are never alone before God, we are always two.

Finally, Christ is *the one whom* we celebrate. Christian prayer is directly related to the very mystery of Christ; this is its essential object. The whole liturgy consists in making reference to the great stages, the great mysteries, in the life of Christ, who has manifested to us the grace and mercy of God, the eternal secrets of his love. The Church recalls these mysteries to God as being *the great reasons why he should listen to us.* This is the underlying theme of each prayer in the liturgy: "You who came to live among us, you who poured forth your blood for us, listen to us." Almighty God, by giving us his Crucified Son and all the mysteries accomplished in his flesh, puts at our disposition the infinite resources of his mercy and gives us power over him. The Office of the Church celebrates her Spouse by commemorating the mysteries by which he gave her his life and continues to give it to her.

Do we not find this act of "commemoration," of "recollection," very often in the Bible? (Exodus 32:11-14; Judith 4:9-15, and 6:18; I Chronicles 16:9, 11, 15; Psalms 105, 106; Esther 4:5; Deuteronomy 9:18, 26; Isaiah 63:7-19; Jeremias 32:20-22) "And now, Lord, God of Israel, you who led your people out of the land of Egypt with your mighty hand, with signs and wonders and great might, and with your upraised arm, so that you have made for yourself a name till the present day" (Baruch 2:11). "Remember at this time not the misdeeds of our fathers, but your own hand and name" (Baruch 3:5). "He who has not spared even his own Son but has delivered him for us all, how can he fail to grant us also all things with him?" (Romans 8:32). Does not the "memory" of everything God has already done become the principal motive for prayer and the great reason for hope?

Is not one of the most profound movements in the prayer of the Mass the commemoration, or recollection, of the mystery of the Redemption: "We remember the Passion of your Son, his Resurrection, his Ascension; we present to you the perfect victim ... and through him, with him, in him, we give you glory."

Prayer will transform our feelings, desires and sufferings into the feelings, desires and sufferings of Christ. This transformation is similar to the one realized in the Mass, when the bread and wine are transformed into the Body and Blood of Christ. We remain ourselves and yet, through prayer, a kind of "transubstantiation" takes place; to a certain extent we acquire a personality infinitely greater than our own. We are no longer alone when we chant the psalms or read Scripture: it is Christ, our eternal High Priest, who chants and reads God's plan of love in heaven: "Thus, in the case of these two (the Church and Christ) everything has proceeded as if there were only one person. . . If they are two in one flesh, why not also two in one voice? Let Christ, therefore, speak, for it is through Christ that the Church speaks; and it is through the Church that Christ speaks. The Head speaks through the Body, and the Body through the Head" (St. Augustine).

Read Chapter 5 of the Epistle to the Hebrews (this entire Epistle is a kind of major "foreword" to the prayer of the Church). The appointment of a Just Man, offering himself and praying for the people, the "recapitulation" in one person of the destiny of all people, are these not already alluded to in all the great examples of the Old Testament? Abraham (Genesis 18); Moses (Exodus 32:32; Psalm 106:23: "Then he spoke of exterminating them, but Moses, his chosen one, withstood him in the breach to turn back his destructive wrath"); Job 42:8; Isaiah 37:14-20.

Is this not the meaning given to devotion to the Lamb by the Apocalypse? Note that it is at the center of all Christian prayer: he alone can open the sealed scroll (see Apocalypse 5:4-10, and compare it to Isaiah 29:10-12, and Luke 24:25-27).

The Only Face God Cannot Ignore

To conclude, we can now understand that if we abide by this great law of prayer, "in the spirit of Jesus," or "in the name of Christ," there will no longer be any opposition between private prayer and public prayer. A resolution is easily made: on the one hand, we will not be tempted to hide ourselves in an individualism that is not Christian ("God and my soul"); nor, on the other hand, in all the community-type illusions that would prevent us from praying without the support of a collective euphoria. Private prayer, like public prayer, is the prayer of Christ: both Christian only insofar as they imitate Christ's prayer, i.e., prayer made "in the Spirit" (Luke 11:13). "But in like manner the Spirit also helps our weakness. For we do not know what we should pray for as we ought, but the Spirit himself pleads for us with unutterable groanings" (Romans 8:26). "Wherefore I give you to understand that no one speaking in the Spirit of God says 'Anathema' to Jesus. And no one can say 'Jesus is Lord,' except in the Holy Spirit" (I Corinthians 12:3).

Whether our prayer is private or public, it is the same Spirit who prays in us, the Spirit of Christ. Every liturgical service conducted in common depends on the personal relation of each of the members to Christ (just as in a choir, the quality of the group depends on the intensity of the relationship between each member and the choir master).

"The sons of God constitute the body of God's Only Son; and since he is the head and we are the members, there is only one Son of God. Therefore, he who loves the sons of God, loves the Father. And no one can love the Father without loving the Son; whoever loves the Son must also love the sons of God ... and through love he himself becomes a member in the union of the Body of Christ, and there will be only one Christ, who loves himself" (St. Augustine).

All this enables us to discover the first concrete movement that governs every Christian prayer, the first call that should open each one of our prayers: "Come, Spirit of God," "Come, Lord Jesus, Come," "Lord, teach us how to pray." *Only God can produce prayer in us*, because in the final analysis *only the love of a God can bring us face to face with God's own love*. It can be said that a person becomes a Christian when he can no longer speak to God except with and through Christ, since he knows that the only face from which God cannot turn aside is that of his Son. "For all you who have been baptized into Christ, have put on Christ" (Galatians 3:27, and also I Corinthians 1:9; Ephesians 1:5; Galatians 4:6).

III

HOW NOT TO PRAY

*"For our glory is this: the
testimony of a good con-
science."*

— II COR. 1:12

*"The one went back justified,
the other did not."*

OBSTACLES AND DEVIATIONS

WE are surprised to see how the Apostles, in the discourse after the Last Supper (John 14:9) as well as during the Agony (Mark 14:37), despite several years of living with our Lord, remain "novices" in the area of prayer. And yet, who can say that he actually *knows* how to pray? In confronting the mystery of God, we will always remain "apprentices." We must be conscious of all the obstacles, all the difficulties, that compel us to say again and again: "Lord, teach us how to pray." What are the chief obstacles?

— *lack of poverty;*
— *lack of preparation;*
— *lack of disinterest.*

LACK OF POVERTY

Illusion of the Cerebral

We think that in order to pray we must have ideas. Have we not often said to ourselves that our prayer was not good because we did not "come up with any ideas"? "I am so little inspired when I pray." Do we not then resemble a fiancée who says to her beloved: "Wait a minute, what you are saying interests me; I want to take notes." When we approach God, we are not taking in a theology course, or presenting a dissertation, but conforming our will and our plans with his will and his plan of love.

Let us take the psalms as a model: they consist of a very small number of elementary ideas that scarcely vary in their expression: divine grandeur, human weakness, divine mercy, human trust. To appreciate the psalms does not require unusual intelligence. Was Christ looking for "something rare" when he invited us to pray: "Come to me, *all* you who labor and are burdened"? To be invited to the Lord's table, it is enough for us to be in a state of need. Recall, for example, the astonishing simplicity of the peasant who was asked by the Curé of Ars, who was intrigued by the man's frequent visits to Church, what he said to Christ during his long periods of prayer: "Well, Father, I don't tell him anything... I catch a glimpse of him and he catches a glimpse of me! "

Prayer is a language of the heart, which is, first of all, in the realm of faith, of a point of view: "Thy will be done." Every meditation must bring us to this point; otherwise, it is still only an expression of our own sufficiency. Learn to look and to be looked at, to love and to be loved. This does not mean that we must always start with a minimum of ideas or thought to avoid a wandering of the mind, and in order to hold it firm and express what will enable it to find Him from whom we might be separated by distraction. But meditation — this effort of the mind and imagination — must always be marked by the desire to encounter God and to make this will and his love our own. It is a search for the living God. We do not pray in order to improve our talents, to develop more clearly an intellectual synthesis, or widen our culture, religious or otherwise. We pray in order to tell God once again that we love him and know that he loves us, and to relate ourselves to the plan of mercy that is his.

Illusion of the Sensible

We run still greater risks in the realm of sensibility, and in believing that our prayer has value only when we have "felt" something. The modern world takes special interest in "experiences," descriptions, states, of the soul; there is a kind of cult for everything that can yield some kind of "interior witness." We delight in working out a projection of ourselves that arises from the senses.

Prayer is an extremely favorable opportunity for realizing such a projection. But this will always be the great difference between Christian and non-Christian prayer: the former does not contain its own end. A person does not pray primarily in order to find himself, but to give himself, to enter into a plan of salvation that *goes beyond himself.* In Christian prayer, what matters above all is not the quality of the interior experience, which can sometimes be very shallow, but the Person who is the "object" of this experience. St. Paul speaks of "groanings" (Romans 8:26) or of a "cry" (Galatians 4:6). What is important, is not our experience but the gift we make of ourselves. We should enter into prayer, not to receive, but to give, to give ourselves and lose ourselves. And if friendship with God is to remain pre-eminent in our prayer, we must enter into prayer in order to give ourselves as a free gift, with the knowledge that we may not always really give what we are giving, and yet without being concerned about what we are giving. We should read again the parable of the Pharisee and the Publican: the Pharisee is convinced, but the Publican is not sure, that he is bringing to God the most beautiful gift possible, by giving God the opportunity to manifest his goodness. In our own day, it would almost be pharisaic to say, "I've enjoyed making you happy," since this might indicate that it was the self that was the focal point in the particular situation, for example, the giving of a gift. To be able to give, and to know that one can give, is still the mark of a wealthy person.

But What Do You Want to "Do" in Prayer?

Christ tells us: "Blessed are those servants whom the master, on his return, shall find watching." If we really pray under the impulse of love, we agree to wait until the other Person wants to give himself to us and share with us what surpasses us and will raise us to a higher level: his plan for the world, his work. But if we go to another person, first of all, because it is a pleasant experience, and for what we may get out of such contact, this is not yet love. If we come to God for the interior well-being we are searching for in prayer, this is still not love. *As long as a person does not love "for nothing," he does not really love.*

The apprenticeship of true love presupposes a kind of courage that we too often underestimate. Prayer takes place in the context of faith, and all the saints had to hold firm in view of a certain silence on God's part. But they understood that this silence was only an indication of the real quality of divine love; because he loves us, God does not want people to be deceived over him, to be satisfied with impressions. Therefore, he invites us to analyze and surpass our impressions within the context of our prayer. God does not want us to merely hold on to past graces; we must "gather the fruit and throw away the branch." The important thing regarding gifts of grace, is the effect they have on our lives, rather than the enjoyment they may bring. St. Francis de Sales does not conceal the courage needed to overcome the illusions we may have about prayer: "You tell me you do nothing in prayer, but what do you want to 'do' in prayer other than present over and over again to God your state of wretchedness. The best way in which beggars can appeal to us is when they reveal their misery and needs. But according to what you tell me, you sometimes do nothing of the kind, but 'remain there like a shadow, a statue.' People only put statues in palaces in order to satisfy the eyes of princes. If you are satisfied doing this in God's presence, he will give life to the statue when he feels like doing so."

Is it not always an inordinate concern for one's plans, ideas and preoccupations that prevents a person from heeding the call and invitation of Christ (Luke 14:16-24)? Concerned with his own "ego," a person is not in a *state of listening.* But what does Christ ask? That we "open the door" to him (Apocalypse 3:20), and then he will bring everything to us. Only they shall finally enter the banquet hall, who have heard the call and who "were waiting." But only those who are truly aware of their poverty wait in the proper way (Luke 14:21-23).

Are not intellectual effort, "the attempt to acquire ideas," the search for self and the need "to feel something," symptoms of a lack of faith, in the sense that a person prefers intermediary signs rather than the actual reality of the mystery? (Cf. I Kings 18:16-40, for a comparison between the prayer of the priests of Baal and the prayer of Elias; the priests of Baal were reported to "feel" something.) Notice the way God punishes a lack of trust, for example, when the people in the desert grow tired of the manna and demand meat (Psalm 77:29-31 and Numbers 11:4-34). While the coming of the angel is already a response to the prayer of Zachary, what the angel says is not enough for him, for he needs a sign; he does finally get one ... by being struck dumb (Luke 1:8-20). On the other hand, God comforts a person's faith which has been tried and which does not seek its own ends (see Elias, I Kings 19:4).

Are we not sometimes too concerned about knowing what we are giving God, knowing whether it was a "beautiful" Mass, a "beautiful" prayer? This is normal, as long as it does not mean seeking out our own ends. Are we not often tempted to know precisely and to measure the value and even the success of our prayer in a very incomplete way?

LACK OF PREPARATION

Another danger threatens our prayer: the illusion of believing that we are always prepared to encounter God. It is actually a twofold illusion: first, our heart is concerned about something, and so we are not in a state of

silence. Secondly, we really are unfamiliar with
the ways of God. A lack of silence and interior
purity, and a lack of knowledge about doctrine
are two obstacles that stand in the way of preparing ourselves for prayer.

Lack of Silence and Detachment

"It is not the road that hurts your feet, but
the pebble that you have in your shoe" (Arabian
proverb). The main obstacles in life come from
within, although we tend to accuse what is
outside of us: our neighborhood, our job, our
standard of living. How can we claim to be at
rest? It is our interior life that we should be
concerned about. "I put aside the concerns of the
world, source of a thousand problems, but still I
could not abandon myself. I am like those travel-
ling by sea, who in ignorance of the crossing,
experience nausea and malaise because they are
unhappy with the ship, which seems to roll too
much. Then passing into a fishing boat or launch,
they experience nausea and malaise at every
moment, for their annoyance and anger have
stayed with them. Thus it is with us: bringing
along the passions which are lodged within us, we
have the same problems everywhere, so much so
that we would not profit very much by going
into solitude. What should be done, is this: 'If
anyone wishes to come after me, let him
renounce self' " (Letter of St. Basil of Caesarea
to St. Gregory).

In our prayer, we pretend we have come to
listen to God and to share his plan of salvation,
but we are too weighed down with ourselves and
spend our time in talking about our own plans.
The Curé of Ars compares Christians who go to
Mass, unprepared, to a sponge that a person dips

into a very pure liquid without having previously taken the trouble to wring it out.

Are we not inclined to interpret silence as being but the mere absence of words or external sounds? Should we not also include everything that weighs us down, "the pebble that you have in your shoe," everything that is hard to put aside, or is of no value?

We could, therefore, meditate on the question of silence, by honestly considering each of the following points:

1. *Our "Memory"*: the internal bitterness, rancor, temperamental acts, points of honor, the remembrance of everything that did not conform to the idea we had of ourselves and of all this internal denseness. "When will you accept peacefully the trial of not pleasing yourself? At that moment, you will make room for Christ" (Letter of St. Theresa to her sister).

We often resemble a child who returns to his mother after a long absence and who, having passed through the door, notices that his shoes got rather dusty from the road and goes out again to wipe them off, instead of throwing himself into the arms of his mother who is waiting for him. *Very often in our prayer, do we not let ourselves be seized by the memory of everything that troubles us?*

2. *Our Character:* Another source of interior difficulty results from all the ideas people form about us. We attach great importance to the image others have of us. We resemble the pigeon, about whom animal psychologists speak, who seems to be happy and healthy only when he has his companion near him. Such psychologists have

conducted the following experiment: isolating a pigeon in a cage one of whose walls consists of a mirror. The animal is perfectly happy as long as he feels his partner is with him; the "other" animal thus serves as a reflection of the first animal's image.

In a similar way, we are concerned with those around us, and are often forced to play a particular role, in search of the image that will reassure and flatter us, and give us the satisfaction of an artificial peace, i.e., an imaginary one. "I have nothing," Abbé Chevance liked to say. "It took me thirty years to realize that I had nothing, absolutely nothing. What overburdens man, is his dreams" (Bernanos, *Joy*).

3. *Our Activity:* An excessive concern for one's work, a desire to achieve quickly results that can be seen, can lead to a certain fear, a fever, a kind of activism, that ruin our prayer. This internal tension is carried over into prayer itself; thus, the effort to get rid of distractions becomes, in itself, another distraction. Some people have become incapable of taking time out to pause in their busy lives (cf. the case of people forced to retire: men incapable of living without their work). *Is this our situation?*

4. *Our Passions:* All our little interests ("Whether the bird is attached by a cable or a wire, it is attached," as St. John of the Cross said), our manias for well-being or perhaps an exaggerated attachment to a person.

All this arises when we are victimized by a *love of ourselves.* But *one type of love is not replaced simply by another type of love.* If love means no longer being anything but one with the beloved, this can take place only if a person is free of attachments to anything else. Loving someone, means preferring him to everything else. We would not accept a love that did not want everything, that did not demand being preferred to everything else. This is the meaning of "internal silence": *silence as a waiting for love.* It is the great means and also the sign whereby we return to our original vocation: to be beings open to the sharing of eternity, beings whose most profound duty is to be in a *state of waiting.*

Silence, recollection, i.e., the positive bringing-together of ourselves, produces one of the great benefits of prayer: the unifying of our life. What exhausts the soul, and is one of its great sufferings, is the inevitable multiplication and dispersion of the tasks that a man must assume. It is by repetition that we complete our work and ourselves. Because of this dispersion, we are constantly in search of our real center of gravity, which we cannot find amid our impressions. If the focal point of our actions is ourselves, we will forever remain in the realm of the discontinuous and diverse. Only silence can bring unity and permanence to our lives, since it elevates us to a point higher than ourselves; it involves a waiting for love, and causes us to look for support in the only place that is stable: the will of God.

We should not, however, minimize the difficulty of such recollection; so many practices of the modern world move in opposite directions and cause us to avoid ourselves, to refuse all solitude and to engage only in small talk. In such circumstances, a person must always start all over again. The conditions of life will never change this, and when we try to establish calm within us, we experience distraction and discover how far this absence of silence can lead us. It is normal that this effort should be difficult, because

circumstances are opposed to it and we ourselves
do not know what we really need.

Christ, however, is extremely emphatic about
this: "But I tell you, that of every idle word men
speak, they shall give account on the day of
judgment" (Matthew 12:36). Christ thus states
the first condition of prayer: "But when thou
prayest, go into thy room, and closing thy door,
pray to thy Father in secret" (Matthew 6:6). We
can expect nothing from our prayer if we are
unfaithful to this effort of interior silence, and as
long as we are not convinced that in the world
we must be "our own milieu." Insofar as the
modern world no longer provides an external
framework based on Christian truths, it is up to
us to create the proper atmosphere and to
acquire habits of living so strong that they will
bring about the atmosphère our soul needs.

Lack of Familiarity with Doctrine

A person only waits for that which he knows;
and the more he knows it, the longer he can
wait. The best way to avoid the "waltz of the
imagination" and the "desire to get away from it
all" (and thus one of the many ways to find
silence) is to concentrate on something stable,
such as the truth. Why do we sometimes feel so
"far away" in our prayer, if not because we are
unfamiliar with the concerns of God? Our prayer
is often anemic because it lacks nourishment. Let
us not confuse spontaneity and carefreeness. Our
love will not be less spontaneous because it refers
to doctrine. On the contrary, claiming to love
someone you do not know, can mean remaining
in a state of purely sensual affection; a love is
truly "spiritual" only if it prefers knowing someone else to experiencing its own emotional satis-

faction. To avoid the tyranny of egotism in prayer, one of the best ways is never to neglect intellectual preparation. We must always conform our desires and interior drives with what Scripture and Doctrine tell us are the great desires of Christ and the Church.

...ist of passages from ...starting-off points ...e, how the Church ...and books of the ...m of the liturgical

...must be convinced ...emptiness can be ...concrete. Why not ...could have at our ...ctrinal ideas which ...he great interests of ...is life?

...contradicts what we ...ng prayer a form of ...n opportunity for ...maintain a balance ...ctual prodigality (a ...g to each person's ...ho truly loves, it is ...asleep or of taking ...barriers between the ...at constitute prayer; *...reading and medi- ...they lead us toward*

IMPRIME EN ITALIE
PRINTED IN ITALY

° *The plan of God:* Ephesians 1; I John 3-5; John 17.
   The life of God: John 14-17; I John; Isaiah 60-66.
   The gift of God: Philippians 2; Colossians 1; John 1; Hebrews 5-10; Isaiah 53. *The new life:* John 3; Ezechiel 36. *The sacraments:* John 6; Romans 6; Luke 15.
   The kingdom: Its history: Psalms 66, 67; Matthew 13; John 10; Acts of the Apostles. *Its laws:* I Corinthians 13; John 13, 15; Luke 10; Romans 8; Matthew 5-7; Matthew 10.

conversation with God. "When it seems that God is listening to us and looking at us, it is good to be silent and listen; otherwise, we should not remain lifeless and do nothing. This is what happens only too often to the soul; sometimes the more disturbed it is, the less effort it makes to do any thinking" (St. Teresa of Avila).

In the encounter with God, we should know how to be silent, rather than continuing to meditate on ideas. But in case of distractions, we must also know how to come back, like a man on a springboard, to what we were doing before, reading certain passages or pursuing an idea that led us into conversation with God. Guigues the Carthusian once said: "Reading, meditation, prayer, contemplation are all related. What's the sense of reading unless we absorb all the flavor of the work and mull it over to the point of its affecting the depth of our heart? Likewise, what's the sense of seeing, in meditation, what we must do if this is not followed up by a request for God's grace? Such fervent prayer ordinarily - brings about the pleasure of contemplative dialogue."

Read again the parable in Matthew 12:11: It is not enough to hear a call, a person must prepare himself and purify himself. (Cf. Genesis 4:3-5; Isaiah 1:10ff.: the strong invective against the lack of interior dispositions. Genesis 35:2-5: one cannot pray without divesting himself of all his idols. Josue 7:6-15: the same severity of God. Psalm 49:7-23: "Not for your sacrifices do I rebuke you, for your holocausts are before me always." Michea 6:6-8.)

A solution is given by Matthew 5:23-24 (note the preciseness of Christ's words): not, "if you have anything against your brother," but, "if your brother has anything against you." But who can claim that there is even one person whom he has not offended?

Note the misfortune of all those who are unprepared for the coming of Christ: the foolish virgins (Matthew 25:1-13), the servant (Luke 12:35-48).

The role of silence in prayer: cf. Apocalypse 8:1; Wisdom 18:14-15 (when God appears to Elias); I Kings 19. There is neither thunder nor storm, but only a "murmuring." See also Isaiah 30:15; Matthew 6:6.

God alone can prepare us. Do we think about this often enough? And are we convinced that the act of praying is already a grace, which must be asked for? Read once more the account of the great vision and encounter of Isaiah, 6:5-7; and the reaction of St. Peter, Luke 5:8-9.

LACK OF DISINTERESTEDNESS

Just as the world in which we live is hardly conducive to silence, it has also acquired the habit of judging everything by the return it brings. Technology — and the idolatry it can lead to — drives us to making of everything some kind of a tool and to accepting only "that which can be used for something." Gratuitousness is what distinguishes most clearly spiritual love from animal love. The animal ceases to desire when it gains possession of its prey; as for man, once the desire is assuaged, love does not become less, it unites itself with the object of its love. It is then the love, not of the beggar, but of the one who possesses. A man then moves on to discovering the perfection in the other person and to a *love of pure benevolence*: I no longer love someone else only because he fulfills my need, but having discovered his greatness, I know he is worthy of

my admiration. Above and beyond the use it can
bring me, I enjoy giving honor to what in him
attracts me, and this fact guarantees that my love
will continue.

Man alone can render homage; it is this that
gives a radiant quality to his poverty as a
creature. Such homage is no longer that of a
beggar who begs for what he needs, but a feeling
of admiration for everything the other person is.
It is not because I need God that I adore him,
nor because he is stronger than I, but because he
is *worthy* of being adored and receiving my
homage. But if adoration is born only of fear or
a desire for something, it will always be a
reaction due to weakness. "Worthy art thou, O
Lord our God, to receive glory and honor and
power," said the angels and elders of the Apocalypse (4:11).

This should eliminate from our prayer any
attitude marked by calculation. It is one of the
clearest signs that distinguish the soul of a poor
man from that of a rich man: the latter receives
and gives in a calculating way, and in fact lives
on calculation. The *really* poor person does not
calculate.

Nevertheless, the fact remains that very often
we view prayer as one of many other means at
our disposal. *Are we not tempted to take refuge
in prayer, like someone who has recourse to a
final maneuver after having tried everything else?*
Then we transform God into a "means" of
rendering us service, and endeavor more or less to
use him.

In complete opposition to this are the kinds of
prayer that aroused Christ's admiration the most,
for example, that of the holy woman, Madeleine,
who carried the alabaster jar (Mark 14:3-6): likewise, David dancing before the ark. On the other

hand, Judas' complaint leads to a reprobation
from Christ, and Mikal, daughter of Saul, is
inflicted with sterility on account of her mockery
(II Samuel 6:16-23). We should enter into prayer
with the conviction that it is not a means similar
to others, but that we enter into it in order to
abandon and lose ourselves. Prayer should
develop in us a "sense of the useless," of
"gratuity," which for man is the best proof that
his love is not a mere animal-type love. It is
essential to prayer that it persevere, that it
persevere in love, and that it transcend our needs
in order to attain the state of disinterested
pleasure in the God who is loved.

Read Mark 9:22 for the statement of our
Lord, "If thou canst believe. . ." Do we not often
have the same attitude as the father of the
possessed boy? We are not very sure that prayer
will help, but we can always try it, just as a
doctor would make a last effort with a new
medicine. If no good results from prayer, it still
will not do any harm.

Judith 8:10-27, and 9:5-6: Are we not often
tempted to pray only when we need something,
such as at examination time or at the threat of
someone wanting to leave us? At such a time, we
are praying more or less on condition. . .

Amos 4:4-5 and 5:21-23; Osee 8:11 and
10:21; Michea 6:6-7: Note the sternness of the
Prophets when a person tries to "assure himself
of" divine benevolence. One "does not use" God.

Amos 9:1-3; Osee 10:7-8 and 12:12; Michea
3:12; Ezechiel 11:4-12; Jeremia 7:1-5. Similarly,
a person does not use the promises of God or his
temple to be assured of some kind of magical
protection. In opposition to this magical attempt
of "assuring oneself," of taking hold over God,

read again the examples of gratuitous acts (Mark 4:3-6).

READINGS

LEARN TO PRAY WITH YOUR WEAKNESS

When you began your petition, an answer was given which I have come to announce, because you are beloved.

— Daniel 9:23

You say you do not do anything in "prayer," but what do you want to "do," if not what you are doing, i.e., presenting and re-presenting your wretchedness to God?

When God rubs something out, he does so in order to write something in its place.

— Bossuet

The saint prays with his experience and the sinner with his sin.

The work that God does in us is rarely what we expect. The Holy Spirit almost always seems to act the wrong way and to waste time. If the piece of iron could picture the file that is slowly wearing it down, what anger and annoyance it would feel! This is the way that God works on us.

— Georges Bernanos, *Sous le soleil de Satan*

He, then, that seeks pleasure in aught else keeps not himself empty that God may fill him

with his ineffable joy, and, in the state in which
he goes to God, even so does he go out from
him, for his hands are encumbered and he cannot
take what God gives him.

> — St. John of the Cross, *Letter to the
> Discalced Carmelite Nuns of Beas*
> (November 18, 1587), in *The Com-
> plete Works of Saint John of the
> Cross*, translated and edited by E.
> Allison Peers (Westminster, Md.:
> Newman, 1949-51), vol. III.

Unless he is completely blind, the blind person
does not allow himself to be completely led by
his guide; but insofar as he can see, he believes
that the first road he comes upon is the best
since he does not see any better ones. In this
way, he can lead astray his guide, who sees better
than he; for after all he is the one who gives the
orders rather than his guide. Likewise, if the soul
depends upon its own knowledge, its own way of
experiencing or feeling God — how very small
these are and how unlike what God is — in going
on its way, it can easily get lost or else come to a
halt, unless it is completely blind in its faith,
which is its true guide.

> — St. John of the Cross, *La montée au
> Carmel*, trans. P. Cyprien de la
> Nativité (Desclée de Brouwer, 1949).

I should regret having slept (for seven years)
during my prayers and acts of thanksgiving — but
I do not regret it... I recall that little children
please their parents as much when they sleep as
when they are awake, and that when performing
operations doctors put their patients to sleep.

Finally, I recall that "the Lord is aware of our fragility, that he remembers that we are only dust."

> — St. Theresa of the Child Jesus, *Histoire d'une âme* (chap. VIII, Mss. A 75, verso 176).

And when I asked her to teach me how to pray, since my soul yearned for it, she could not believe that being in the religious state so long I did not know how to do it. But when she was convinced of this, she told me for the first time: "Go put yourself before God like a canvas that awaits a painter."

But I wanted her to explain this to me, for I did not understand her, but I did not dare tell her so; but I heard these words: "Come, I will teach you." And as soon as I was at prayer, my sovereign Master showed me that my soul was a canvas-in-waiting, on which he wished to paint all the strokes of a life of suffering, and that he would make his own impressions after cleaning it off.

> — St. Margaret Mary, *Vie par elle-même* (De Gigord, 1934), no. 36, p. 47.

One day a disciple met his master and said to him: "Master, I want to find God." The master looked at the young man without saying a word and smiled at him.

The young man came back each day and repeated his desire to pursue a religious life. But the master knew better than he what should be done.

One day when it was very warm, he asked the young man to accompany him to the river for a swim.

The young man dove into the water. The master followed him and deliberately held him under the water. When the young man struggled for a moment, the master released him and then asked what he wished for most when he was under the water:

"Air," replied the young man.

"Do you desire God in the same way? " said the master. "If this is how you desire him, you will find him instantaneously. If you do not have this desire and this thirst, you will struggle in vain with your intellect, your lips and your own strength, and you will be unable to lead a religious life. As long as this thirst is not aroused in you, you are not much better off than an atheist. Besides, the atheist is often sincere, while you are not."

Hail, blue abyss! you are the Frontier, the region that is midway between a place and that which is not place, time and that which is not time.

Just as the vase and the bellows exist with their emptiness, like a lute,

Just as the hub of a wheel, where the joints meet and by means of which the wheel turns, is empty,

So all things contain some part of your emptiness.

> — Paul Claudel, *Le repos du septième jour* (Mercure de France, *Théâtre*, IV), p. 122.

A sculptor does not make a piece of sculpture, he takes away whatever is covering it up.

How can God enter your heart if there is no room,

If you do not make way for him? . . .
Who can put liquid in a vase that is no longer
there?

> — Paul Claudel, *Cinq grandes odes*
> (Gallimard), p. 166.

A brother who had renounced the world and
had distributed his wealth to the poor, keeping
very little for himself, came up to Abbot
Anthony. Aware of this, the older man said to
him: "If you want to become a monk, go to the
village, buy some meat and put it around your
nude body and then come back." When the
brother had done all this, the dogs and birds tore
apart his body. When he came to the old man,
the latter asked if he had taken his advice. When
the other man showed him his body, St. Anthony
said to him: "Those who have renounced the
world and want to keep some wealth, are similarly attacked and are torn to pieces by demons."

> — Apophthegm of the Fathers, Abbot
> Anthony

God does not consider what one gives, but what
one keeps.

> — St. Ambrose

PRESERVING ONESELF FOR THE UNIQUE

Once upon a time, Sen Rikyu, the grand
master in charge of the arrangement of flowers
and the ceremony of tea, was cultivating asagao
(which are bindweed, convolvolvus, a rare,
imported flower in Japan). The emperor

Hideyoshi (a great statesman and warrior) announced to Sen Rikyu, then out of favor, that he would come see his field of flowers.

When he came, all the flowers had been cut, and the field was empty. Hideyoshi at first thought this was a new affront on the part of his former favorite, who had once refused his daughter, and anger grew within him.

"Be patient," said Sen Rikyu to him, and he brought the emperor into a room for the ceremony of tea. In the tokonoma he put the only specimen that had not been cut. "If you had seen all the other flowers," said Sen Rikyu, "you would not have had as much pleasure as looking at this one."

(So it is with us: If we scatter our love in a number of directions, we make no effort to preserve it for one person in particular.)

— Japan, 16th century

I have put aside the cares of the world, source of a thousand misfortunes, but I have not yet surrendered. I am like people on the ocean who, inexperienced in travel, experience nausea and confusion; dissatisfied with the ship, which seems to them to roll too much, they then move on to a fishing boat or a launch, but disgust and anger continue to influence them.

The same is true of us. Carrying with us our passions, our perpetual "tenants," we experience the same annoyance wherever we go, so that we do not gain much in solitude. What is needed is this: "If anyone wishes to come after me, let him renounce self."

— St. Basil of Caesarea, *Letter to Saint Gregory*, 2, A and B

A few poor fish dealers, surprised by a violent storm, took safety in the garden of a rich landowner. The latter received them warmly, gave them a meal and let them rest on a huge veranda, in the midst of gorgeous flowers that perfumed the air. The women laid down in this scented paradise, but could not fall asleep. They lacked something that was part of their life, and they could not do without it.

At last, one of them arose, went to where they had left the fish pails and brought them back to the veranda. Satisfied with the odor that was familiar to them, they soon fell into a deep sleep.

May the world and its sins not be our pail of fish!

For neither is a sublime communication of him or a sensible revelation of his presence the clearer testimony of his presence, nor is aridity or the want of all these things in the soul the less clear testimony thereof. For which cause says the Prophet Job: *Si venerit ad me, non videbo eum; et si abierit, non intelligam* [Job 9:11]. Which signifies: If He (that is to say, God) comes to me, I shall not see Him; and if He goes away, I shall not understand Him. Wherein is to be understood that if the soul should experience any great communication or knowledge of God, or any other feeling, it must not for that reason persuade itself that it possesses God more completely or is more deeply in God, nor that that which it feels and understands is God in His Essence, however profound such experiences may be; and if all these sensible and intelligible communications fail, it must not think that for that reason God is failing it. For in reality the one estate can give no assurance to a soul that it is in His grace, neither can the other, that it is without it. As the Wise Man says: *Nemo scit ultrum amore aut odio dignus sit* [Ecclesiastes 9:1] . Which is to say: No mortal man can know if he be worthy of the grace or of the abomination of God.

> — St. John of the Cross, *Spiritual Canticle, Stanza I*, in *The Complete Works of Saint John of the Cross, op. cit.*, vol. II.

TAKE OFF ONE'S SHOES

When Moses tried to draw closer to the burning bush, he was prevented from doing so as long as he did not take off his shoes. And you, who want to see Him who surpasses all thought and feeling, will you not rid yourself of every idea derived from the senses?

> — Evagrius, *Traité de l'oraison*, no. 4

Unfortunately, our heart is not free or cleansed of every earthly affection. Take a very dry, clean sponge; dip it in liquid, and it will fill up to the point of overspilling. But if it is not dry and not clean, it will not absorb anything. Similarly, when our heart is not free and unattached to earthly things, we have trouble dipping it in prayer, and so it absorbs nothing.

> — Curé of Ars, *Catéchisme* as cited by Monnin, *L'esprit du Curé d'Ars* (Téqui, 1935), p. 48.

Like animals tied to a post, who can move only as far as their rope stretches and who, when untied, can then turn around only with great difficulty, many souls labor considerably in that

most difficult of human acts, namely prayer.
Thinking they are doing the right thing, they
constantly introduce obstacles to divine activity,
and following the usual custom of meditating on
a few specific ideas, they limit themselves in the
choice of subject matter and do not deviate from
their usual way of reflection.

> — Jean-Joseph Surin, *Le catéchisme
> spirituel* (Bouix, 1882), p. 100

When the sun is hidden, the stars come forth.
One day, a holy man stopped at our house. My
mother saw him in the courtyard, doing sommer-
saults to amuse the children. "Oh! " she
exclaimed, "he is truly a holy man. My son, you
may go out to him."
He put his hand on my shoulder and said to
me, "Little boy, what do you intend to do? "
"I don't know. What would you have me do? "
"No, say what you want to do."
"Well, I like to play."
"Then do you want to play with the Lord? "
I didn't know what to say. He added, "You
see, if you could play with the Lord, that would
be the greatest thing that was ever done. Everyone acts so seriously toward him that he turns
out to be quite unexciting. Play with God, son.
He is the best kind of playmate."

> — Gopal Mukerji

A long speech is one thing, a long love
another.

> — St. Augustine

Jesus was sleeping as usual in my little skiff.
How rarely souls allow him to sleep peacefully
within them. Jesus is so tired from always

opening himself out to people and bearing the
cost that he hastens to take advantage of the rest
I offer him. He will not wake up, I trust, before
my entrance into eternity.

> — St. Theresa of the Child Jesus,
> *Histoire d'une âme*, chap. VIII, Mss.
> A, folio 75, verso

It is not the road that hurts your feet, but the
pebble that you have in your shoe.

> — Arabian proverb

TAKE NO REST

One of the most graphic images proposed to us
by the Bible concerning our attitude in prayer is
that of keeping watch like a sentry. "Upon your
walls, O Jerusalem, I have stationed watchmen;
never, by day or by night, shall they be silent. O
you who are to remind the Lord, take no rest
and give no rest to him, until he re-establishes
Jerusalem and makes of it the pride of the earth"
(Isaiah 62:6-7). But a sentry must heed demands
that can be severe. Read again the extraordinary
Chapter 33 of Ezechiel and the discourse of St.
Paul (Acts 20), "I am innocent of the blood of
all."

Night has always been a special time for
prayer.

THE WORST THING IS TO GIVE UP

I think much credit in the sight of God is due to
a friar of the Order of Saint Dominic, a very
learned man, for it was he who awakened me

from this sleep; it was he who, as I think I said, made me communicate once a fortnight, and do less that was wrong. I began to return to my senses, though I did not cease to offend the Lord, but, as I had not lost my way, I continued upon it, first falling and then rising again, and making very little progress; still, he who never ceases walking, and advances all the time, may reach his goal late, but does reach it all the same. To lose one's way seems to be the same thing as giving up prayer.

> — *The Life of the Holy Mother Teresa of Jesus, op. cit.*, chap. 19

Faith means continuing to pray in the night because for the one who prays there is no night that does not finally bring forth its own dawn.

If your servant says to you: Sir, for two years, following your order, I brought a candle every morning — at five o'clock in wintertime — to your son so that he could get up and study, and yet he did nothing but let it burn on the table and slept every day until seven o'clock.

Then you should tell him: In that case, don't bring it to him anymore.

(Pay heed to God, who passes by every morning and will perhaps grow weary if you continue to sleep.)

> — Père l'Aveugle

Whoever draws close to the Lord must first purify himself if he has not yet received from the Spirit the gift of prayer. Seeing him struggle and punish himself for the sake of the good he seeks, even if he does so somewhat unwillingly, God will grant him the true prayer of Christ, bowels of mercy, a true goodness — in a word, he will bestow on him the fruit of the Spirit.

— Ps.-Macaire, *Homélie 13*

Sometimes with little effort you will pray well; at other times, after great efforts, you will not achieve your goal. This is so that you will try harder and your conquest will then be inviolable.

— Evagrius, *Traité de l'oraison*

The brothers then questioned him in this way: "Father, in life, what virtue requires the greatest effort?" And he replied to them: "Believe me, nothing seems to require more effort than praying to God. For every time a man wants to pray, enemies try to deter him from it; they are aware that a person can resist everything if he prays. Whatever kind of virtuous life a man pursues, he will find satisfaction if he perseveres in it; as for prayer, a struggle is required up until the last breath.

— Apophthegm of the Fathers. Abbot Agathon

LET ME ALWAYS PURSUE YOU

As much as I could, as much as you allowed me, I pursued you; I wanted to see by the light of intelligence what I believed; I studied much and struggled hard. O Lord, my God, my only source of hope, listen to my prayer lest through fatigue I no longer wish to pursue you, but allow me always to pursue you with ardor (Ps. 104:4). O God, give me the strength to seek you out, you who made me to find you and have given me the hope of finding you again and again. You know

my strength and weakness; maintain my strength
and cure my weakness. You know my knowledge
and ignorance; where you have drawn me to,
receive me when I wish to enter in; where you
have stopped me, open up to me when I come to
knock. Let it be you I remember, you I understand, you I love. Increase these gifts within me
until you have completely formed me anew.

> — St. Augustine, *De Trinitate*, I, IV,
> VIII, 12 (trans. Mellet-Camelot, t. 15)

The best advice to follow is not to become
discouraged and not to stop praying because you
do not get the feeling of devotion you would
like. . . Our soul is like water that has been
agitated. All efforts to quiet it down will prove
of no avail; only time and tranquility will bring
back to the water its original limpidity.

> — Louis of Grenada, *Livre de l'oraison
> et Méditation* (trad. Vivès, 1863), XI,
> p. 229.

At Raphidim, Amalec came and waged war
against Israel. Moses, therefore, said to Josue,
"Pick out certain men, and tomorrow go out and
engage Amalec in battle. I will be standing on top
of the hill with the staff of God in my hand." So
Josue did as Moses told him: He engaged Amalec
in battle after Moses had climbed to the top of
the hill with Aaron and Hur. As long as Moses
kept his hands raised up, Israel had the better of
the fight, but when he let his hands rest, Amalec
had the better of the fight. Moses' hands, however, grew tired; so they put a rock in place for
him to sit on. Meanwhile Aaron and Hur
supported his hands, one on one side and one on
the other, so that his hands remained steady till

sunset. And Josue mowed down Amalec and his
people with the edge of the sword.

— Exodus 17:8-13

THREE TIMES, TEN TIMES, TWENTY TIMES

O woman! (Matthew 15:28). God said, "O
woman! " Listen, all you who do not know how
to pray. When I tell someone: Pray to God,
beseech him, implore him, people say: I prayed
to him once, twice, three, ten, twenty times, and
I never received an answer. Brother, do not stop
until you have received what you seek; the end
of prayer is the gift one asks for. Stop when you
have received it, or, rather, do not stop but even
then continue on praying. If you have not
received an answer, ask that you may receive one;
if you have received one, give thanks for what
you have received. Although you may be outside
the Church, say, cry: "Have pity on me." Do not
simply move your lips, cry out with deep understanding. Even those who remain silent are heard
by God. What counts here, is not the place but
the fact that a person is beginning to correct a
situation. . . If you are taking a bath, pray; on a
trip, in bed, no matter where you are, pray. You
are the temple of God, do not be concerned
about the place where you may be; only the
desire that you have is important.

— St. John Chrysotom, *Homélie 10, Sur
le renvoi de la Chananéene* (M.G. 52,
457)

In this area . . . the principle is similar to the
one that pertains to a balancing act at the circus:
in the beginning the effort required is a normal

one; everyone can do that part of it. But at a certain point in the act, when the acrobat is in a horizontal position, the operation becomes serious; he is far from the center of gravity, and the latter weighs heavily upon him. What special effort is required to come to a vertical position, the head down, and, having passed the "midpoint" of the balancing act, to turn around? Brute force does not suffice. What is needed here, is continual effort, steady, coordinated progress. "Coordination" is the word — coordination is the cause of success. The most difficult thing — the main difficulty — is when you are within a hair's length of the end: at the critical moment, a buckling may take place. But if one overcomes this, he is on his way. However, many people do not overcome this hurdle.

You are too bashful and timid in your request for money, from a father who wants to give it and when you have greeted me with a letter such that I would not only repay each line of it with a gold Philippeus (as Alexander did with Choerilos), but, if my means were as great as my desire, I would reward each syllable with two ounces of gold. As it is, I send only what you have asked, but would have added more, except that as I am eager to give, so I like to be asked and coaxed by my daughter, especially by you, whom virtue and learning have made so dear to my heart. So the sooner you spend this money well, as you always do, and the sooner you ask for more, the more will you be sure of pleasing your father.

> — *Letter of Thomas More to His Daughter Margaret*, in *St. Thomas More: Selected Letters*, ed. Elizabeth Frances Rogers (New Haven: Yale University Press, 1961).

It is difficult to burn green wood, but with a strong puff it will take fire and begin to glow amid dark smoke. Little by little the fire increases, the humidity of the wood is absorbed, the smoke grows thinner and the fire, casting a bright glow, rises victorious and crackles in the pile of faggots. . .

But when everything is consumed and the wood is completely taken on the appearance and properties of fire, all noise and crackling cease. . . The fierce, devouring fire, after having affected and consumed everything, remains in a state of peace and silence, because it no longer finds anything different from or opposed to it. Thus the stages of a fire illustrate what also happens to our soul in the course of prayer.

— Hugh of St. Victor

PRECEDE THE DAWN

Paul and Silas have taught us that the middle of the night should be devoted to prayer, as the Acts tell us: *"But at midnight Paul and Silas were praying, singing the praises of God"* (Acts 16:25). And the psalmist likewise says: "At midnight I rise to give you thanks because of your just ordinances" (Psalm 118:62). We too must precede the dawn and wake up to pray so that the day will not seize us in our sleep and in bed, as the psalmist suggests: "My eyes greet the night watches in meditation on your promise" (Psalm 118:48). Those who have resolved to do everything to obtain the glory of God and of Christ should not leave any of these moments pass.

— St. Basil of Caesarea, *Règles plus développées* (Answer to Question 37, 5)

· Therefore, do not let the night be a special
time reserved for sleep. Do not allow the insen-
sibility of sleep to render useless half of your life.
Divide the time of night between sleep and
prayer.

> — St. Basil of Caesarea, *Sur le martyre
> Julitta, Homélie 5, 4.*

One must set aside a certain number of hours
to devote himself in a special way to God. The
best thing is to devote the morning to this concern, to exert oneself in a spiritual exercise as if
one were training for an athletic contest. Every
day, at a specific hour, pray in the most secluded
part of your house and keep your room closed.
Make a desert for yourself, and, to some extent
away from the world, unite yourself more in-
timately with God; once you have returned to
the other people in the house, show what fruits
you have gathered from reading and prayer. In
this moment of solitude, your chief concern
should be to nourish your soul as much as it may
need for the entire day. Read the Scriptures and
remember always that it is the word of God,
demanding not only knowledge but the
fulfillment of its law. There is not much point in
learning what you should do, if you do not do it.
Let your reading be frequently interrupted by
prayer, and let your soul, ever attached to God,
be inflamed with an intelligent response to these
holy works.

> — Pelagius, *Épitre à Démétriade, 23*

As for setting aside specific times for prayer,
nothing has been stipulated except that one pray
at all times and in all places. But what does "all
places" (I Timothy 2:8) mean? The Apostle says,

wherever the occasion presents itself or the need compels you... As for setting aside specific times, it will not be useless to observe certain hours. Do not pray less than three times daily in honor of the Father, Son and Holy Spirit, to whom we owe what we are; this would be apart from our required prayers, which without any reminder we should make morning and evening. But it is also fitting that the faithful should not eat or go bathing before having said a few prayers. For the spirit must be purified and nourished before the body, and heavenly things should pass bofore earthly things.

— Tertullian, *De la Prière*, chap. 23

It is said that the brothers in Egypt have certain prayers which they recite often, but they are very brief, and are, so to speak, darted forth rapidly like arrows, so that the alert attention, which is necessary in prayer, does not fade and grow heavy through long-drawn-out periods. By this practice they show quite well that, just as this attention is not to be whipped up if it cannot be sustained, so, if it can be sustained, it is not to be broken off quickly. Prayer is to be free of much speaking, but not of much entreaty, if the fervor and attention persist. To speak much in prayer is to transact a necessary piece of business with unnecessary words, but to entreat much of Him whom we entreat is to knock by a long-continued and devout uplifting of the heart. In general, this business is transacted more by signs than by speech, more by tears than by utterance.

— St. Augustine, *Letter to Proba*, in *Saint Augustine: Letters, The Fathers of the Church* (New York: Fathers of the Church, Inc., 1953), vol. II.

Is it a desire? A thought? A feeling? Put aside such questions, for they are useless. Instead, ask: Is it really He? Is it really me? Is it really His will for me?

The soul should forget itself and forget what it is doing, for (as one Father of the Church has said) prayer is perfect when a person does not realize he is at prayer.

— St. Peter of Alcantara

Please consider the fact that the Lord calls everyone (to prayer)... If his banquet were not for everyone, he would not summon all of us... But I repeat, he makes no restrictions. Yes, he summons all of us.

— St. Teresa of Avila, *Chemin de la Perfection, Oeuvres complètes* (Ed. du Seuil), p. 363

How long do you halt between sides? If the Lord be God, follow him.

— I Kings 18:21

IV

THE PRAYER OF CHRIST

*Never Speak without Him,
and He Will Never Say
Anything without You.*

— St. Augustine

*"When you pray,
say: Our Father"*

ORIGINALITY OF CHRISTIAN PRAYER

Our Lord did not have to pray for the same
reasons that we do. In a certain sense, he did not
need to pray at all. But he wanted his prayer to
serve as an example for us. He himself stated that
was the reason why he prayed. Thus, after having
the stone rolled back from Lazarus' tomb, he said
before the crowd: "Father, I give thee thanks
that thou hast heard me. Yet I knew that thou
always hearest me; but *because of the people
who stand around, I spoke, that they may believe
that thou hast sent me*" (John 11:41-42).

See Yourself in Me

Does this mean that Christ prayed only with his
lips, that he pretended to pray, as if he simply
wanted to offer himself as a kind of grand
gesture? Certainly his human intelligence did not
have to "ascend" toward God, since he could
always see his Father: "The Father never leaves
me alone." But in praying before his disciples,
our Lord wanted to authenticate for us the truth
of his Incarnation, to make clear to us that he
had assumed a human nature, with all that is

included in the incarnate: sensibility, passions, affectivity and his own emotions. And he prayed with all this sensibility, in a humble and completely human way, stirred to tears at the death of his friend Lazarus (John 11:35-38), disturbed at the weakness of St. Peter (Luke 22:32), overwhelmed with anguish before his own cup of sorrow (Matthew 26:39).

One of the great purposes of his prayer is to *reassure us*. "Yet not as I will, Father, but as thou willest": Christ showed us that at certain times, because of his instinctive desire, man sometimes desires what God does not. Our Lord really wanted to reassure all those who, after him, would be troubled by weakness, death, a strong passion, by showing them that he also experienced this and had prayed under the same circumstances. "Christ-made-man gives, as it were, an example of a man's personal will when he says: 'Let this cup pass away from me.' In effect, this was a human will wanting its own good; but since he wants to be an honorable man, a just man, as he had to be before God, he adds: 'Yet not as I will, but as thou willest.' *It was as if he were saying to each one of us:* 'See yourself in me'; you yourself can actually wish something, although God may wish the opposite" (St. Augustine).

Thus, by his prayer, Christ made himself our model. He also wanted to reassure and encourage us by confronting all the difficulties and vicissitudes we could encounter. Still, he did not want to be a mere teacher of religious conduct, but wanted to specify the very words we would have to use in order to please God, his Father. Promising an answer to all prayer made in his name, he wished to teach us not only the attitudes for such prayer, but also the great moments for it and its long-range progression. For this reason, we shall now try to discover the important stages in prayer, its development, and also the reason why Christ chose certain words with which we might address his Father.

First, then, we will see that prayers are arranged according to the three movements characteristic of all prayer, although we should not establish an arbitrary division between them. In the same act, prayer includes *praise, adoration* and *petition.*

Next, we shall try to understand the originality of such prayer, and why, in its perfection and efficaciousness, it is the only kind that the Father cannot resist.

All this will enable us to understand how the prayer of the Church in her liturgy is but the continuation and extension of the prayer of the Lord.

THE THREE MOVEMENTS
IN CHRIST'S PRAYER

All the prayers of our Lord which the Gospels record are very similar in their structure, development, choice of words even, as well as in their progression. This is especially evident in the two main prayers: The *Our Father* and the *Priestly Prayer.* We can summarize in three phrases their different movements, their progression, and hence that of all Christian prayer: "Father" — "Your Name" — "Your Kingdom."

Our Lord's prayer arises from an acknowledgment of the gift of God that inspires *praise* and *thanksgiving*: "Father." But this gift, manifesting the greatness of the Father, leads to *adoration*: "Your Name." Suggesting at the same time the extent of this gift and the poverty of those who receive it, the audacity and effect of this prayer prompts a petition: "Your Kingdom."

Starting with the Priestly Prayer (John 17), try to discover the similarity of the stages in all the prayers of our Lord. They are always preceded by an invocation of the Father and begin with an expression of thanksgiving. Read John 17:1-8. Then comes the invocation of the Name: John 17:6, 11, 12, 26. Finally, the prayer for the Kingdom: John 17: 9-26; with the detail of that intercession for the Kingdom which the *Our Father* and the *Priestly Prayer* call for: on earth as it is in heaven (John 17:4-5); asking not to be led into temptation (John 17:12), and to be delivered from evil (John 17:15).

We can establish a parallelism not only between the *Our Father* and the *Priestly Prayer*, but also between the *Our Father* and a great many of our Lord's gestures and words, thereby showing how the *Our Father* expresses the basic sentiments of all prayer. Note the following similarities:

Father: Matthew 11:25-26: I praise you, Father, Lord of heaven and earth. John 17:4-5: I glorified you on earth.

Your Name: Matthew 11:25: I praise you for what you have revealed... No one knows the Father except the Son. John 12:28: Father, glorify your name. John 17:6-11: I manifested your name to men; keep in your name those whom you gave me.

Your Reign: Luke 17:20: The Kingdom of God does not come in a way that dazzles the eyes. John 18:36: My Kingdom is not of this world. Luke 10:11: The Kingdom of God is close at hand.

Your Will: Luke 22:42: Let not my will but thine be done. Hebrews 10:7: This is why I come, Father: to do your will. John 4:34: John 6:38.

Our Bread: Matthew 6:25: Do not be concerned about what you will eat... Luke 11:9-13: Ask ... which one of you will give a stone to his son if he asks for a loaf of bread.

Forgive me: Matthew 18:21-22: up to seventy-seven times seven — the parable of the two debtors (Mark 11:24-26). Luke 23:34: Father, forgive them...

Temptation: Luke 22:31: Simon, Simon, I prayed for you so that your faith would not fail. Matthew 26:41: Watch and pray in order not to enter into temptation — John 17:12.

Evil: Mark 9:29: this kind of demon can be driven out by no other means but prayer. John 17:15: I do not pray that you take them from the world, but that you preserve them from evil.

Note also the similarity between these three moments of our Lord's prayer and the greatest prayers of the Old Testament, e.g., those of David (II Samuel 7:18-29) and Tobias (Tobias 13:1-23).

"Father"

Above and beyond all the titles they attributed to Christ, such as Messias, King, Prophet, etc., the apostles, and especially St. John and St. Paul, present him to us emphatically as the "one sent from God," the personal "gift" of God to men. "Yes, God so loved the world that he *gave* his only Son, so that every man who believes may not perish." And St. Paul remarked: "He who did not spare his own Son and *delivered him up* for us, how can he not grant us all the rest? "

Christ is, above all, the Son given to the world. Therefore, his prayer is addressed necessarily to the one from whom he proceeds, the one who sent him: The Father. It always begins with an invocation of this paternity, which, in God, is the source of what he is for men. Thus, our Lord teaches us to whom we should address our prayer: He to whom we pray is the Father, and more exactly "the Father of our Lord, Jesus Christ." The Father is the One who sent him, and who gave him to the world. It is from his grace, grace as Son and First-Born, that his prayer arises. "As my Father loved me. . ." He to whom our Lord prays is the One who showed his love for men by a gift: the gift of the Son given over to us in the Incarnation. This explains why the first movement of this prayer involves an act of thanksgiving, praise, a "blessing," with all the nuances that such an invocation can have: from amazement at the gift made to the little ones (Luke 10:21-22) to ultimate confidence (Luke 23:34-36). In such an act of thanksgiving, St. Paul summarizes all prayer: "And because you are sons, God has sent the Spirit of his Son into our hearts, crying, 'Abba, Father! ' " (Galatians 4:6 and Romans 8:15).

"Your Name"

But this gift is a grace, for in its origin it is pure generosity, pure gratuitousness. God is not enriched in any way when he communicates himself. He does not need to give himself in order to perpetuate or complete himself. While the giving of self, the communication of all the excellence one has, brings an increase of perfection to every finite being, since by this gift he extends and prolongs himself in other beings — an obvious increase for a creature, i.e., someone who is limited — God is the only one who does not acquire any perfection in giving himself. For God is unlimited happiness, to which nothing can be added. And since, as God, he is perfectly sufficient unto himself, he is the only one who acquires nothing in the giving of self. Therefore, he is also the only one who can give himself "for no reason." The gratuitousness and generosity of his gift are signs of the purest love, of the only pure love, for we *"are of no use"* to God. Such generosity and gratuitousness are the clearest proof of his divine uniqueness, transcendence and dignity. On the other hand, man always has a certain interest in his love, even in the love that gives itself to another.

In considering the strictly divine aspects of the Father's gift and discovering the magnificence implied in such a gift, we see that Christ's prayer is one of adoration. Within his own being Christ, so to speak, discovers to what extent this gift not only proceeds from the purely gratuitous initiative of the one offering it, but also confers titles to be received. By his own virtue he compensates for the delays, weaknesses or imperfections that are an obstacle to him. For he addresses himself to the impious: "While we were still sinners. . ." The gratuitousness of the gift is born of mercy, and comes from the One who both gives and pardons, who can make himself smaller than the being he saves since he has no fear of being destroyed. Only that which is perfect can give itself to what is spotted, without risking corruption. Only He who made the law can grant pardon. Only He who is almighty power can control his own strength and remain master of himself in love, and in the presence of offenses. Only He who is all love can take the initiative of giving himself up and offering himself as ransom, "the first" to accomplish the process of reconciliation, and thereby proving the right to adoration that the Almighty and Merciful One enjoys.

> "It is right and just to praise you, holy and
> all-powerful Father, and through Christ to
> to adore your majesty, to reverence it. . ."

says the Preface in the Mass, repeating the hymn of the Apocalypse:

> "You are worthy, O Lord God, to receive
> glory, honor and strength. . ."

Are we not often tempted to visualize God's reactions on the basis of our own and to abstract from such reactions his divine character? Socrates, a pre-Christian, warned his disciples when false objections were being made against the mystery of God: "Take care not to blaspheme the immortal gods."

Do we not feel we have said everything about God when we have spoken about his power of forgiveness and opposed it to his justice? Here again, let us not forget the true nature of his generosity: God is not the way we want him to

be. We believe we have done everything when we
pardon someone who has offended us: God, on
the contrary, weeps with the sinner and comes
and takes his place, even going so far as dying for
him. Transcendent in his generosity, the God of
Christians is the Complete Other, even after he
has drawn close to us.

Is not our prayer too often addressed to an
abstract, deformed image, to a God as the re-
presentative of an idea and a law, much more
than to the ineffable Person who, through his
love, has allied his destiny with ours? Are we
aware of the full meaning of God's name? Are
we not too quick in thinking that we are not
guilty of all these shortcomings? Read Numbers
20:2-13. Faced with the criticism of the people,
Moses himself has doubts about divine generosity.
It is not because he strikes the rock twice that he
will be punished, but because he suggested to the
people that there were limitations to God's mercy
and goodness: "Because you were not faithful to
me in showing forth my sanctity before the
Israelites, you shall not lead this community into
the land I will give them."

In contrast with this attitude, note how St.
Paul and St. John love to emphasize divine
gratuitousness as the most characteristic sign of
God's love, and which is the strongest reason for
our adoration and the source for our hope.

"And hope does not disappoint, because
the charity of God is poured forth in our
hearts by the Holy Spirit who has been
given to us. For why did Christ, at the set
time, die for the wicked when as yet we

were weak? [Follow closely Paul's reasoning here.] For scarcely in behalf of a just man does one die; yet perhaps one might bring himself to die for a good man. But God commends his charity towards us, because *when as yet we were sinners, Christ died for us. Much more* now that we are justified by his blood, shall we be saved through him from the wrath. For if when we were enemies we were reconciled to God by the death of his Son, *much more*, having been reconciled, shall we be saved by his life." (Romans 5:5-10)

Read also I Timothy 1:15-16; Titus 3:5; Ephesians 2:8, and also Romans 9:16: "So then there is question not of him who wills nor of him who runs, but of God showing mercy." Is this for us, as for St. Paul and St. John, a mystery, *the* mystery, the secret of God? Read once more St. Paul's great hymn to God's benevolent love for us, a love hidden for centuries (Ephesians 1), and discover in the apostles' words what should be the source of joy for the adoration of Christ: the fidelity and superabundance of the Father's gift. Cf. Ephesians 1:3; John 10:10; Romans 8:31-39.

"Father, glorify your name." "Let your name be made holy." Christ knew that by praying so that the honor of which the Father is worthy might be given to his name, he was praying in order that the real character of the Almighty's transcendence might at last be recognized, that is his mercy. He also prayed in order that finally, and under his real name, we might call upon the only One who could bring us salvation: God-who-is-love.

"Your Kingdom"

Having rendered honor and glory to the name of
the Father from whom every gift comes, Christ
intercedes for his Kingdom. After thanksgiving
and adoration, the third movement in his prayer
is petition. Realization of the extent of God's
gifts increases the desire Christ has to see them
shared and received by those entrusted to him.
Having received his faithful ones from the Father
(John 6:37-44), his first concern will be to keep
them under his Father's protection (John 10:29).
This is the whole concern of the second part of
the *Priestly Prayer*, as it is of the second part of
the *Our Father:* "I pray for them; not for the
world do I pray, but for those whom thou hast
given me, because they are thine..." (John
17:9-10). But they will find themselves alone
when Christ departs, hence the request: "That
they may be one even as we are" (*ibid.*, v.11);
"Keep them from evil" (*ibid.*, v. 15), and
"Sanctify them in the truth" (*ibid.*, v. 17).

Aware of the price of the Kingdom, since he
himself is the ransom whereby it has been
acquired, Christ concludes his prayer by pleading
fervently for all those who are called to take part
in the Kingdom.

Jesus specified a certain number of requests
which he wanted us to make on our own:

— *the Kingdom of God and his justice:*
Matthew 6:33. Justice means here sanctity, and
summarizes the practical working-out of the
Beatitudes — laws of the Kingdom which will be
taken up again in the *Lord's Prayer:* forgiveness,
etc.

— *the Spirit of the Kingdom:* Luke 11:13.

— *workers for the Kingdom:* Matthew 9:37.

Do not all the requests that can permeate our prayer go back to the twofold request that sums up all the religious aspirations of the Old Testament: seeking the face of God and preparing for his reign? Longing for the face of God becomes in the New Testament the "call to the Spirit," a gift of God, who in turn discovers his own face in the heart of the Christian (II Corinthians 4:6 and 3:18). As for the expectation of, and preparation for, the Kingdom, in the New Testament these are the ultimate concern of Christ's soul, as is revealed in the requests of the *Our Father.*

Does this not suggest one of the great *specific demands* of our prayer? In view of everything we could desire, should we not simply ask ourselves: *What relationship does this have with the Kingdom?* In this not also the essence of the *unity* of our prayer, the fundamental aspiration that will give it internal coherence: establishment of the reign of God?

But do we not live too often in a state of false idealism, believing that this reign of God is foreign to the concrete circumstances of our life? But consider the example of Christ: his concern for all mankind and for each and every man. Nothing in the suffering of those around him is foreign to him (see the Appendix for a list of the specific occasions of his own prayers and of those addressed to him). There do not exist two separate universes, one for our private life and the other for prayer, with the latter alone working in conjunction with the Kingdom of God. On the contrary, everything that makes up our life — our duties, the smallest worries, the most accidental meetings, the moments of weakness — all this is the Kingdom if through prayer we can *give it existence in the eyes of God.* On certain days, the best way to "make" our prayer will perhaps be simply taking our day's schedule, or else repeating in advance what we will do throughout the day, and offering each of our actions to God. What connection does this or that have with Christ? What is Christ's wish in this matter or that? Can I have this or that, in view of my life in common with Christ? The simplicity of prayer and of the Kingdom: a hidden seed and ferment.

PERFECTION OF CHRIST'S PRAYER AND ORIGINALITY OF THE CHRISTIAN'S PRAYER

Our Prayer and That of Christ

Our prayer takes substance within the context of Christ's relationship to his Father. This is what constitutes the originality of "Christian" prayer: *it is derived completely from a gift of Christ.*

It springs from recognition of this gift, this grace that comes from the Father of our Lord, Jesus Christ. It gains support from the manifestation of this gift to rise to the divine secret which it symbolizes and to adore the goodness that is its source. Thereafter, it dares to ask that this gift should continue until the Kingdom arrives.

Because the *initiative* in this process is *divine*, and is manifested in Christ, we can claim to have access to the true God. We cannot raise ourselves to God's level by "boosting ourselves up," but as the Church says after the Canon of the Mass: "Taught by our Saviour's command and formed by the word of God, we dare to say: Our

Father." "In order that God might be praised by man, God praised himself," St. Augustine says: "in order to be praised by his servants, he filled them with his own Spirit, and since it is his Spirit that praises him in his servants, is it not he himself who sings his own praises? " By the gift of Christ, God brings us, so to speak, into his monologue, into the marvelous secret of his design (reread Ephesians 1). Therefore, insofar as we adopt the desires and "sentiments" of Christ, our desires become, through an amazing reciprocity of love, the object of his decrees of eternal love, and collaborate with the working-out of his plans of mercy.

Thus, prayer is *Christian* only when it effects this substitution of wills in the context of love, and, at the same time, finds its perfect model in Christ's own prayer.

Is it not because he realizes perfectly the gift he represents for men that Christ prays for them, and invites them to take up his prayer? Read again John 17, and compare it to the Preface of the Mass and the part of the Canon that follows the Consecration: "In memory of the blessed passion ... resurrection ... we offer up to your resplendent majesty, from your own gifts bestowed on us, the sacrifice that is perfect. . . Through him, and with him, and in him, is to thee ... all honor and glory. Therefore, we dare to say: Our Father. . ."

Perfection of Christ's Prayer

If the completely new element in Christianity is the realization that God invites us to share friendship with him (John 15), to enter into charity with him (and thus with each of those who are his image), this friendship will be real only as long as it tends toward a perfect reciprocity, i.e., an absolute conformity of wills, and only if the other person really becomes "another me," i.e., if his existence, desire and will become law in me. But, by ourselves, we can lay no claim to this unless we are introduced into it by Christ (Hebrews 6:17-20, and 8,9). This is the most profound characteristic of his prayer: to be the *expression of a perfect friendship,* the response on earth of the perfect love of the Son for the Father.

For us, the only infallible way of entering into perfect friendship, perfect reciprocity, perfect conformity with divine love, which the Spirit calls for in our hearts, will be to identify ourselves with the desires of Christ. Therein will be effected that would have been unthinkable by our own strength: Our prayer will overcome its limitations and will be clothed in the perfection of Christ's prayer, with its boldness and its universality.

Such prayer bestows courage, assurance and infallibility. Only Christ could say to the Father, "I will" (see the end of the *Priestly Prayer,* John 17:24) and pray with complete dependence on the Father since to him alone have all things been given (John 3:35). He alone is spared of doubts, certain of the absolute efficaciousness of his requests since he is the only intimate friend of the Father and he alone knows perfectly what Providence has allotted to his prayer. This enables him to communicate his assurance to those for whom he has prayed (e.g., St. Peter: Luke 22:32) and arouse their confidence: "But even now I know that whatever thou shalt ask of God, God will give it to thee" (John 11:22-42). Thus, the peace and filial confidence of Christ, as well as his boldness, also become ours.

Along with this confidence and peace, our prayer will receive from Christ's its *magnanimity* and *universality*. Through his prayer, it is united to the redemption of all mankind. Experiencing the despair of the world, we can relate it to the distress of Christ in his Agony; sharing the joys of other men, we can transform them into the hymn of the Resurrection. Only Christ's wishes correspond fully with those of the Father, and through such wishes our own can share in the concern of "all the Churches" and the establishment of the Kingdom in its fullness. "My God, grant that all men may go to heaven," Charles de Foucauld used to say at the end of his catechism lessons in the Sahara.

In view of the misery and distress that we meet and for which we can do nothing, do we really *believe* (for it is a matter of faith) that it is up to us to direct everything back to God? Are we convinced that we can transform the distress of the world by prayer? Or do we only let ourselves be overcome by the powerlessness that we experience, by the feeling that "there is nothing to be done," before so much sadness, banality, the impossibility of solving anything, or before problems whose basic elements escape us, at least in part (social injustice, imperialism, war)? And do we not sometimes depend to some extent on forgetfulness ... instead of making our prayer one of real commitment and a means of getting involved to some extent in a particular situation?

The gift God asks of us, is the gift of his Son because this is the gift he gave us, this gift which is the Holy Spirit himself. God needs our love, just as he needs his Son; it is not a matter of choice, now that he has determined it — and he determined it for all eternity. Thus, when we cease to love God, God to some extent loses his Son, and when we come back to him, he regains his Son. We thus possess the very real power of giving him his Son by what we do; if we refuse, a gift of the Son to the Father is not made, although the eternal gift cannot cease. "I called you friends because everything I learned from the Father, I made known to you." God has only one love, and when he loves, he can only give that kind of love. The Father wants to revive in us what takes place between himself and his Son. This is, in the last analysis, the ultimate secret of our prayer and his perfection.

V

THE PRAYER OF THE CHURCH

Watch, then, praying at all
times, that you may be
accounted worthy . . . to
stand before the Son of Man.
— LUKE 21:36

*"Where two or three
are gathered together
for my sake. . ."*

A METHOD OF PRAYER

Experienced monks tell us that to avoid all
discord in a religious community, two subjects
should not be discussed: politics and . . . the
liturgy. Is this true only of the religious life?
Then try in a parish to introduce only a few
changes in the celebration of the Mass. What a
chorus of protests you are liable to cause!
People are either *for* or *against*. And sometimes is
this not also our own attitude toward the liturgy
and common prayer of the Church? Some people
want to reduce all prayer to this type, while
others are opposed *a priori* to such a move and
are always ready to accuse every new attempt as
being contrary to "tradition."

Must a person, then, be a romantic or a
sentimentalist to uphold the right of private
prayer, and an esthete or a progressive to love the
liturgy?

WHY A COMMON PRAYER?

Every living being needs an environment in which
to grow. This is not a matter of choice. The

smallest thing, a disturbance in the atmosphere, a change of temperature, are enough to destroy life. The frost of spring, an unusual drop in temperature on a May evening, and the harvest is destroyed.

The same is true for the most important and most fragile part of man: his divine life. Man is not able to breathe in every kind of atmosphere. There are places that are without sun, or else without heat, that only leave the soul in the midst of a desert.

A Way of Life

The Church's liturgy is, first of all, that: a way of life, the atmosphere created by the life of Christ, by the Epiphany of God, in order that this life might be born and grow within man. The Christian community offers an environment that shows men how to live according to the ways of Christ, who assists, supports and illuminates the heart of man.

Just as I do not invent my life, I do not invent my faith but instead receive it as it is. Likewise, I do not have to invent my prayer, but I receive Christ's prayer, born of the Spirit of God and already existing in the community of his sons. The older people introduce the little ones to the life of Christ; the previous generations educate and admit the new generations into this movement of prayer born of Christ and supported by the fact that he is waiting for us.

An environment is needed for the flourishing of every kind of life. Despite the testimony of some (for example, films on religious ceremonies), it is not enough to assimilate the liturgy to the folklore of a village, the customs of a community, the traditions of a family or profession. No, much more is required: a living environment, circumstances that will allow the person who wishes to live to breathe, grow and nourish himself. If the environment disappears, so does the life.

We now have the opportunity to live in a marvelous period of liturgical renewal. The marvelous Constitution on the Liturgy voted by the Vatican Council invites us to renew our hope, our trust and our needs. The example of Pope Paul VI shows us that this is not simply a concern for esthetes, but a challenge to every man's conscience. The liturgical renewal demands of each person patience, attentiveness, precision, and the abandoning of certain small habits, tastes or personal drives.

It is true that there are still immense gaps between the language with which we are asked to pray (what nonsense must sometimes be uttered in the name of renewal!) and the highest part of our sensitivity and heart. *Very little is possible*, for our good will often becomes exhausted and weak; we must be aware of this and accept it calmly, each in his own way. St. Paul knew this when he spoke of "groanings." But what is possible, must be done, beginning with a struggle against all pomposity in order to learn, gradually, how to be authentic.

Let us simply cite the complaint of Claudel which summarizes all too well so much of the inadequacies of our liturgy:

"In our meetings with God, why would not a clean, unspotted place be used, and why do we need all this luster and mountings, these iron grilles and carpets, this crowded bazaar aroung us, which reminds us only too well of the frightening disorder of our heart and memory, these undignified splatterings on the walls, these sinister catafalques, this confusion of filth and sweetness and these flaccid stories spoken everywhere in nasal tone by abominable sacristans? Will we accept indefinitely the regime of plaster and filth? " (*Positions et Propositions* II, p. 216).

Everywhere, that which is alive is in control of its environment. The strong have responsibility for the weak. This is also true of the life of prayer. No doubt, it is often the young who recall and demand the essential things, and the fervor of the new members revivifies that of the older ones. But it is also from the fidelity of the older members that the newly arrived draw truth, or else lose it.

The meaning of the liturgy, the "reason for" common prayer, can be summarized in this way: The Church is able to offer me the prayer of Christ and to welcome me into a living environment, a community, where this prayer can originate and grow.

Thus, it is no more a matter of choice for a "member" to live attached to his organism or to separate himself from it than it is for a Christian to do without his community. A man is Christian only if he is a member of Christ, and he is a member of Christ only if he receives within himself the life that comes through communion in faith and the prayer of his brothers.

Look at the example Jesus himself gives us: He acknowledged the worship given to God in the temple. See Luke 2:46; Matthew 23:21; Mark 11:17; John 2:15-17. He himself takes part in the worship of the Synagogue: Luke 4:14-17 and 13:10; John 18:20.

He agrees to belong to a real community; he recognizes the customs and traditions of Jewish worship and the community meals required by rite (cf. all the accounts of the preparation for the Last Supper; on this point, read Louis Bouyer, *The Meaning of Sacred Scripture*). He also recognizes the Jewish priesthood: Mark 1:44; and the Law: Matthew 5:17; and, finally, the authority of the leaders: Matthew 23:2-3. This is not a simple external recognition; our Lord accepts this religion in a truly internal way (Mark 7: 1-23).

The spontaneous reactions of his prayer constantly give evidence of this. After every great moment in his life, he makes use of the Psalms, which he learned and accepted from the community (see Appendix).

What then, does the early Christian community do? It remains associated with the temple: Luke 34:53; Acts 2:46, 3:3, 5, 25, 42, etc. It preserves most of the Jewish practices, which have finally acquired a precise meaning since Christ adopted them. Christian prayer, therefore, will be misunderstood unless it is seen as being related to a community, a liturgy — that is, in a proper sense, the working-out of a people — but as it is completed and lived by Jesus. It is no longer a matter of choice; Christ has decided for us the kind of prayer he wants. Do we ever reflect on our doubts about prayer conducted in common? Beyond laziness or our own meager well-being, are there not more fundamental obstacles? A false kind of angelism or illusion: the belief that we do not need to learn and to receive from others the nourishment of prayer, the manna? Or else ignorance or, worse, a mere external, abstract knowledge that is contemptuous of things and liturgical signs, which, however, are so simple, real and close to us and are justified not as a kind of theater, even a pious one, but as the living, active presence of a saving God?

Expression of One's Love

A second reason explains the necessity of prayer conducted in common. Let us take the artist as an example. Why does he need to "realize" outside of himself his feelings and enthusiasm? Why did the deaf Beethoven still feel the desire to present to the public the symphony he would no longer hear? If not for the unavoidable need to bring to life, to incarnate and share, an interior enthusiasm and admiration. The same applies to prayer conducted in common: it is, first of all, the expression of an *interior* life, an *interior* soul. It comes from the fervor of a soul that loves, just as the Creation was born in divine love from a need to share. Otherwise, "public" prayer is nothing more than a kind of imitation theater. Actually, it exists both to induce one to internal prayer and to *express it.*

Even though I do not have to invent, but must rather receive true prayer, as a gratuitous gift from above — the prayer of the living Christ which I learn through his Church — it would be an illusion to believe that our role, therefore, is only passive. If the vine gets its life from the sun and the air, it does not grow only because of the sun. . .

A way of life, a teacher of prayer, the liturgy is also — and inseparably so — the expression of my fervor, the external manifestation of an interior transformation and conversation. Thus, we should not reduce the number of external actions that accompany prayer to the pedagogical ends of disposition and formation, as if they were important as a mere prelude to prayer. On the contrary, they not only assure a "milieu" and a "tradition," the formation and transmission of prayer from one age to another, but in a more forceful way translate *the expression and visible incarnation of this homage of my entire self, which is of the essence of prayer*. Without this homage and this interior "devotion," public prayer is only an empty demonstration and, at worse, a lie.

For this reason, Scripture does not limit the liturgy to its earthly manifestations, but on the contrary points to its true center and focal point in heaven, in the liturgy of the Lamb, in the rejoicing of the Apocalypse over the sacrifice of Jesus (cf. Apocalypse 4 and 5, Hebrews 9 and 10). We must however, take note of the change of roles that takes place: In the liturgy, it is not first of all we who "ascend toward" heaven, but it is heaven that makes itself present to us. It is, in other words, the soul beginning its eternal function, its divine "office," the marvelous achievement of its entire earthly life.

Why do introductions to the liturgy — and all that accompanies them, such as the repetition of chants, etc. — sometimes seem so false and artificial, almost like useless games or the concern of esthetes? Perhaps they are too often governed by a mere external consideration, a "community-type" desire, without any interior roots.

Is it not a general law of all our lives that we need external signs — but also that we must master and shape them, in order for them to express what they symbolize, that is, a "spiritual" life? We judge a people by its celebrations . . . and a group by its songs, but not according to the ceremonial or technique alone (cf. the mass demonstrations that take place under dictatorships). Similarly, it would be as false to restrict the effects of prayer, because it is internal, to the limitations of an individual, for prayer surpasses individual actions, as to deny the importance of prayer conducted in common.*

In both private and public prayer, do we accept the prayer of Christ as a source and measure of our own prayer? Do we realize that it is actually senseless to oppose public prayer and private prayer? There is only one kind of "Christian" prayer, viz., the prayer of Christ taken up by each Christian. (Read again Chapter 11, *The Third Law*: "In the Name of Jesus" and Chapter V, *Do We Need a Method for Prayer?*) Public prayer has no meaning or value outside of interior prayer. A man does not lose his personality when he uses an instrument to play in an orchestra; on the contrary, his personality grows larger in the splendor of the ensemble, and vice versa: the group draws its importance from the quality of each instrument and hence each player. Thus it is with our position in, say, a liturgical choir: the latter serves to bring to reality our "private" prayer. If I do not desire to live in Christ, how can I claim to represent him before the world, and to plead the case of my brother before God, in common prayer? (Read again Isaiah 29:11-12, then Apocalypse 5:4-10 and Hebrews 9 and 10).

---

* The Spirit cannot induce me to pray except in the communion of saints. He who led Christ into the desert and directed his ineffable dialogue with the Father has informed us as to how this dialogue included reference to Christ's brothers. We need only read once more the *Priestly Prayer* to appreciate this fact. In meditating upon his Father, Christ was reminded of those whom the Father had given him, who are "greater than all" (John 10:29). Finally, let us note that it is specious to introduce the idea of the primacy of the common good over the particular good to prove that group prayer is superior to private, interior prayer. For truly interior prayer is never enclosed within the limitations of the individual, but rather at the summit of personal activity it is open to the intire community of spirits.

DO WE NEED A METHOD FOR PRAYER?

Common prayer is, therefore, necessary for a twofold reason.

Can we now specify somewhat better its exact relationship to our everyday prayer, our "private" prayer? Briefly, we can say this: *Christ's prayer serves as a model for the Church's prayer, the latter serves as a model and method for our private prayer,* so that there is only one kind of prayer — the prayer of Christ existing in his members.

Christ left us only a small number of prayers. To form its own prayer and relate it at all times to Christ's, the Church takes its model from its Founder and from what the Evangelists tell us about his prayer. We notice that Christ chooses the Psalms as a repertory for his moods. The Church, in a similar way, preserves the Psalms as a remembrance and expression of her Saviour's prayer. On the other hand, the Evangelists show us Christ as realizing in full what had been announced by the great figures of the Old Testament. For St. Luke, he is the new Elias who will go forth into the desert, will be transfigured, will be persecuted because of his witness and finally raised up into heaven. For St. Matthew, he is the new Moses, who will bring to man the definitive law. For St. Paul, he is the new and last Adam who will recapitulate and reunite all people through the gift of a heavenly life. Thus, in the supplication of Elias, the plaint we cry of the Servant of Yahweh, the thanksgiving of Moses, the canticle of Adam, the Church will read and recognize the Eucharist of Christ, the prayer of her Saviour, who will at last bring these prayers to full completion and full reality.

Key to the Liturgy

Here we find the key to all the liturgy. Every occasion (rhythm of the year and of seasons), every text and formula (Psalms, canticles of the Old and New Testaments), every symbol (fire, water, balm, oil, bread, wine), every action (the sacrifice of Isaac, the retreat of Elias or Moses into the desert, the struggles of the prophets, of Jeremias and Isaiah . . .), will prompt us to inquire as to what these realities tell us about Jesus. He himself is the manifestation of God, and the seasons, formulas, history, parables, etc., are but the signs of the activity, life and soul of Jesus. To examine them is to delve a little bit more into his mystery. To study Christ is to know a little bit better what God wants to tell us, through his Son Jesus, who will redeem us and lead us to his glory.

Let us take one example. Thanks to this key to the liturgy, the true meaning of the pascal vigil will be grasped.

To reveal to us the meaning of the thanksgiving, Eucharist, and Passover of Christ, the Church makes use of the series of great canticles of the Old Testament: Genesis, which becomes the canticle of the new Adam, Moses' act of thanksgiving after the Red Sea, the joy of Isaiah, the proclamation of Ezechiel now acquire a new meaning — or rather their real significance is finally made clear: They become the prayer of Christ who fulfills them all completely in the ultimate "prophecy" of the great vigil — the Canon of the Mass.

We Speak in Him, and He in Us

We can apply this to every feast of the Church's year by learning how each Introit, Gradual,

Gospel and Offertory reveal the eternal movements of Christ's prayer and encourage us to adopt them for our own use.

> God could not give to men a more excellent gift than by giving them as leader, his Word, by whom he created all things, and by uniting them to him as his members, in order that he might be both son of God and Son of man; one God with the Father, one man with men, so that when we pray to God, we pray to the Son, and when the Son prays, his body is not separated from its head. Thus our Lord Jesus Christ, sole Saviour of his Body, prays for us, prays in us, and receives our prayers. He prays for us as our priest, prays in us as our head, receives our prayers as our God. Let us then realize that we speak in him and he speaks in us... It is in him that we say, in us that he makes, that prayer of the Psalm entitled the "Prayer of David." Let no one, hearing these words, say: Christ is not speaking here; nor let him say either: It is not I who speak. But if he believes he is part of the Body of Christ, let him say at one and the same time: It is Christ who speaks, it is I who speak. *Never say anything without him, and he will never say anything without you*" (St. Augustine).

Notice how at key moments in his life our Lord chose the Psalms in order to express his feelings.* At the time of his temporary triumph:

---

* In the Appendix, the reader can find a few examples that show how the Psalms are used in the New Testament.

Matthew 21:16; at the last solemn announcement of his death: John 12:27; at the Last Supper, in the face of treason: John 13:18; in the last discourse: John 15:25; and the final prayer: Matthew 26:38 and 27:46. Similarly, the Apostles very often make use of the Psalms to speak of Christ and his prayer: See Acts 13:33, 35; Matthew 27:43; John 19:24, 36; I Corinthians 10:26 and 15:27; Hebrews 10:5-10, etc.

By selecting a few Masses, note how the liturgy uses the same method, and by means of the Psalms appropriates for its own use the prayer of Christ, e.g., the following Masses:

Ash Wednesday: Psalm 29 — Offertory (read the entire Psalm and note verses 10 and 12);

First Sunday of Lent: Psalm 90 — all the Chants (compare Psalm 90 and the Gospel for this Sunday: the temptation of Christ);

Passion Sunday: Psalm 42 — Introit (compare this and the Gospel: the accusers of Christ);

Wednesday in Passion Week: Psalm 26 — Introit (note verses 2 and 9, and compare them to the Epistle: persecuted Daniel as image of Christ).

See the Appendix as to how this method of reading is of value for all the Psalms, and also how we can make more precise the "Christian" meaning not only of the Psalms but of all the books of the Bible according to the way in which the liturgy has emphasized their relationship to the mystery of Christ. Thus, the Psalms and all the books of the Bible can serve as a starting point for our prayer (see the Outline on "The Prayer of the Liturgy" in the Appendix). To take but one example from this Outline, notice the way in which the prologue of St. John, which is the best summation of Christ's life, enables us to

establish more precisely the great stages in the
liturgical mystery. Consider also how the same
book of the Bible can be used in different ways
according to the season at hand. For example,
the synoptic Gospels: After the Epiphany, they
report the "manifestation" of Christ's lordship
(Christ as all-powerful, master of the elements
and of sickness, Judge, etc.); after Pentecost, they
specify in detail the laws of the Kingdom
(pardon, truth, prayer, etc.).

"Never say anything without him, and he will
never say anything without you."

If the liturgy can thus invite us, by means of
the Psalms and the prayers of those who are
already members of the Kingdom, to enter into
the prayer of the One who recapitulates all
prayer the Lord Jesus — it is especially because
he is living, *the* Living One. Victorious guardian
of the secrets of God, he is able to share them
with men, and has appointed himself their
advocate before the throne of God: for salvation
and victory have been won by him — and for all
time.

Necessity and Value of a Method

Such is the liturgical method.

However, we can still be dubious when some
people talk of a "method" of prayer. "Like
animals tied to a post, who can only go as far as
the rope can stretch and who have trouble
turning around. . . A person would not really gain
knowledge of another person if he went to see
him and suggested three points to him, without
going any further." By this excellent example,
Father Surin warns us against the excess of any
method in this area. What Scripture says again

and again (e.g., Ecclesiastes 33:10-11) all the spiritual masters repeat: Nothing could be more opposed to the ways of God than the effort to submit everyone to the same kind of interior gymnastics. Our uneasiness over a "method" of prayer is also founded on this fact: Nowhere should there be greater respect for differences of temperament, background and personal desire than in our relationship with God. So much more so since the essential element here is the encounter of two people, of what is irreducible in God and man, and finally since the essence of prayer life is dialogue, one that is conducted to foster friendship.

And yet, given the disparity of our lives and actions, there is something lacking in a purely negative reaction. It is not enough simply to avoid invitations or temptations to shun silence and to get outside of ourselves. We must not merely maintain a position of waiting for God, of silence and a desire for prayer, by purely defensive reflex actions. More must be done than simply eliminating distractions. We must also nourish this deep desire to meet God so that when the opportunity presents itself, we can take hold of it, and transform every event into an opportunity for genuine dialogue. But the real obstacle to a life of prayer arises from an inordinate love; the Love of self. And the fact is that we do not replace one kind of love simply with another kind. For this reason, we will be fortunate if on certain days we can count on the help of a simple, easy, trustworthy "method."

The value of a method will, therefore, depend on two factors: first, its flexibility, the freedom it leaves us, its "modesty," as it were. It must remain a means rather than an end in itself, and not become a kind of custom-made tool, which is not suited for everybody. Secondly, it will depend on its ability to open out into a dialogue, a Christian dialogue: that of Christ with his Father, and the Church with Christ.

In our relationship with Christ, however, each of us must resolve one great problem: to pass from the abstract level to the personal one, that is, to put aside the kind of relationship that consists largely of ideas one has about Christ and to come to a direct encounter. The same transition points are found in the life of prayer as in any friendship: There is a time when we are still not completely sure of the other person, when we are uncertain as to whether he will think or react like us. Then the moment comes when we are assured of the other person, and every exchange is founded on a personal relationship. Every event and even apparent differences are accepted without fear, since the reciprocity involved is one truly based on love. We love someone else because he loves us. What sustains and activates dialogue is this response, it is the fact that the other person is happy to learn the meaning of our life, and is happy to love us. Therefore, the value of every method of prayer will depend primarily not on the number of abstract ideas it can give rise to, or on any other consideration, but on this fundamental question: Is it a help or a hindrance to the development of an authentic dialogue with Christ?

An Example

We learn for this dialogue with God, this dialogue through Christ. Our first impulse is to try to nourish this life of exchange on the Gospels. But we soon find that something disconcerts us. The Gospels propose *objective* facts, which to us are often *too objective*. The mass of facts and anecdotes have little appeal for us: cures of possessed people, controversies among rabbis, etc., whereas we would prefer to learn somewhat more about the human psychology of our Lord. The same is also true of discourses and sermons: Either they are very complicated, or else are too far removed from our present circumstances, even those that affect us the most, such as the discourse after the Last Supper.

A natural reaction is to attempt to improve our dialogue-in-prayer by works other than the Gospels or New Testament, works that seem to us to be more relevant. This is what undoubtedly accounts for the success of standardized prayers or passages written out in a "dialogue" form. But here, too, there is a problem. Very often, after a period of temptation, these passages, despite everything else, seem rather solemn; a person does not really speak the way they do. They do not open up a genuine dialogue, or else their platitudes and their artificiality seem to mutilate the sense of mystery and no longer present Christ in a way that is sufficiently divine.

In these circumstances, a solution for our "private" prayer is offered to us in the Church's own method, which the Holy Spirit himself has taught and has always urged upon Christians:

— Very simple prayers and always the same ones: the Kyrie, Gloria, Psalms. . .

— But said again each day in the light of a different Gospel.

The Church selects an event from her Saviour's

life and in reading this through meets once again the soul of Christ by entering into the dialogue of his prayers. Thus, by means of these very brief and simple formulas — request for pity, praise, adoration — it begins once again the dialogue of Christ. And this with much variety, corresponding to the diverse moments in our Lord's life, but always related to the unity and simplicity of the *Our Father,* which summarizes everything. (Note how the latter is situated in the context of the Mass: at the conclusion of every prayer of the Canon and as an expression of union with God, which has finally been obtained once again.)

This method of prayer is summarized in one movement:

1. *The Our Father, containing the whole soul of Christ and every Christian soul: Father, Your Name, Your Kingdom*, i.e., praise, adoration, petition.

2. *The Our Father spoken in the light, as made clearer and communicated by a passage from the Gospel.*

Only one question will then accompany every prayer, private as well as public: What does the *Our Father,* spoken by Christ, signify at such and such an event in his life for us who prolong his presence? To "enter into prayer," we have only to open up to a page of the Gospel and let ourselves be transformed by every request of the *Our Father.*

Of these passages in the Gospel, some are points of high interest and will clarify and give meaning to a whole number of other passages. As if in these key passages the light of the Gospel was concentrated in order to be diffused on other passages. Let us select three examples (and the Rosary, with its marvelous intuition, will provide further enlightenment):

The Lord's Prayer at Christmas: God manifests his saving love by taking on a human appearance. Love is love only when it is made personal. God finally satisfies the vow of his love, which is to make himself known as a specific person, in his son, who can manifest him and address him as a Father. This explains the many occasions when Christ is recognized as being the "Son of the living God": for example, Peter's statement: "Thou art the Christ, the Son of the living God... Blessed art thou, Simon Bar-Jona, for flesh and blood has not revealed this to thee, but my Father in heaven" (Matthew 16:13-20 and Acts 2:36). There is also the remark of the disciples: "To whom should we go, Lord; thou hast the words of eternal life" (John 6:68). Consider also the statement of Martha (John 11:25-27); that of the Centurion (Matthew 27:54), like every other "epiphany" (see Matthew 10:32-33; John 1:9-14; Colossians 1,15:2, 9, etc.).

In "private" prayer, let us say the Our Father once again with each of these passages, in the spirit of Christmas.

The Our Father in the Passion: Christ is struck by evil, he grants forgiveness, gives the bread of the Kingdom, prays for deliverance, enters into the struggle for salvation. Grouped together here will be: announcements of the Passion, insults, rejections, scorn experienced by Christ (Matthew 13:54-57; Luke 9:7-9; Matthew 11:20-24; Mark

10:17-22; Luke 13:34-35); calls to penitence and to combat (Matthew 19:23-26; John 12:20-50).

In the same way, we may reflect upon the Our Father in the context of these passages, in the spirit of the Passion.

The Our Father at the Resurrection: It recapitulates all those who were with Christ at every new gift of life: miracles and sacraments, which are but anticipations of the full gift of divine life, resuscitated: the daughter of Jairus (Mark 5:21-43), Lazarus (John 11:1-44), the blind man (Mark 8:22-27), etc., and for the sacraments, for example, the discourses on the bread of life (John 6:22-59), on living water (John 4:7-15; 7:37-39), etc. . .

Thus grouped around the major events of Christ's life, these passages from the Gospels will clarify each other. That which opens them up to our prayer, is and perhaps can only be the soul of Christ, as he himself wanted to reveal it to us in the *Our Father.* No one can say "Jesus is Lord, except in the Holy Spirit" (I Corinthians 12:3); but the prayer of the Spirit is, "Abba, Father" (Romans 8:9-15).

Our book of prayer, which will provide for us our only method, is indeed the Gospels (recapitulating the whole Bible) with all their variety, but transformed into a dialogue through the *Our Father.* This prayer alone harmonizes the life of Christ with all the strains of our soul; it alone can enable us to relate our life with that of Christ. For in every prayer, there is no other way but to "have this mind in you which was also in Christ Jesus" (Philippians 2:5).

The Way of Shepherds and the Way of the Magi

One may say: "And what about the Rosary?"
To this, we answer that liturgical prayer and the
prayer of the Rosary are both prayer. Both are
ways leading toward perfect prayer, which in its
state of ultimate completion is expressed in the
eternal paschal liturgy of the Lamb. The latter does
not pass away; these prayers are not just signs, but
the expression of a superabundance of life and
unity. It is no longer a form of pedagogy. It is
the very song that God himself sings, and that
is sung by men reconciled with the Spirit.

But to illustrate better the place of the Rosary
in relation to the liturgy, allow us to use in an
allegorical way the episode of the shepherds and
the magi.

When the magi arrived before the Infant Jesus,
they learned that the shepherds had arrived much
more quickly than they and at less expense, and
it was only in finding this out that they discovered Christ. . .

And yet it was good that the magi profited
from all the learning and wealth that was
available to them and which was unknown to the
shepherds. For in this way, after having bene-
fitted from all this, they could teach what they
learned to others (St. Paul is an outstanding
example in this regard). It is true that the
shepherd way of life is a poor, impoverished one,
without any kind of glamor.

Now, this is exactly what is offered in the
Rosary, The liturgy which presupposes an ini-
tiation into a language and culture, an apprenticeship and deciphering of symbols, is comparable to
the magi way of life: one had to know how to
read a map in order to find his way. Thus, it is

good that alongside this way there is also another for all those who are unable to benefit from the various riches of a particular culture. We should not separate these two roads. They ascend the same slope, but in different ways. In both cases, it is a question of associating oneself with Christ's prayer, in the way most adapted to our own possibilities, strength and psychology. Everything we have said so far about the liturgy and about the essence of all prayer — the presence of Christ — applies to the Rosary. We should go further, and say that the Rosary has meaning only insofar as it is subordinate to the notion of eternity begun in the liturgy. It is a way that is open to the "shepherds," and yet completely oriented toward the meaning of the eternal as described in the pascal liturgy. It is an orientation that is simply adapted to the lack of culture that will occur no matter what one does, and which is a permanent quality of all who bear witness to "poverty."

Repeat once more with Christ, offering the creation: "Hail, Mary"; say once again with Christ and Mary: "Our Father." And do this throughout the great events that mark the life of Christ and have become necessary steps in the destiny of every Christian. Who can now claim to be above such a "method"? Who can say that he has never experienced in fatigue, sleep, sickness, exhaustion or despair the king of poverty that characterizes a shepherd in the night?

READINGS

SAY NOTHING WITHOUT HIM,
WHO WILL SAY NOTHING WITHOUT YOU

One charge that cannot be made against the Gospels is that they are based on experiences that are unusual or else reserved for the initiated. God reveals himself as a father so often that no one can protest that he has never heard of this. But divine paternity and sonship go beyond all the limitations and inadequacies of human relationships . . . so much so that God himself taught us how to be sons.

If all prayer is based on this divine paternity and providence, the only teacher and paragon of prayer that we have is the one who knows what it means to be a son: Christ Jesus.

Books exhaust me; they contain thoughts of which the ones more beautiful than the other. . . The Gospels are sufficient for me.

— St. Theresa of the Child Jesus

No, sir, neither philosophy nor theology nor rhetoric have an effect on souls; Jesus Christ must exert an influence over us, or else we must cooperate with him; we must work with him, and he with us; we must speak like him and in this spirit, just as he must act through his Father and preach the doctrine that had been taught to him. This is the language of Holy Scripture.

— St. Vincent de Paul

Explaining God to someone after having simply read the Scriptures, is like describing the city of Benares after having only seen it on a map.

In order to be praised by his servants, he filled them with his Spirit, and since it is his Spirit who praises him by means of his servants, does he not sing his own praises?

> — St. Augustine, *In Psalmos,* 26, II, 1

When young Felicity was awaiting martyrdom in prison and cried out in pain when giving birth to a child, one of the jailers said to her: "If you cry now, what will happen in the amphitheater? " And she replied without hesitation: "At that moment, Someone else will suffer within me."

Just as birds have nests in the trees for when they must seek refuge, so must we choose a place each day — on the hill of Calvary, in the wounds of our Lord or some other place close to him — to have a place of refuge for every kind of occasion, where we can refresh ourselves and recreate in between worldly events.

> — St. Francis de Sales, *Introduction à la vie dévote,* II, chap. XII

Here is what you say: Thy kingdom come.
And God cries out to you: I am coming.
Are you not afraid?

> — St. Augustine, *op. cit.,* 66, 10

Behold, I stand at the door and knock. If any man listens to my voice and opens the door to me, I will come in to him and will sup with him, and he with me.

> — Apocalypse 3:20

NOT I, BUT YOUR
UNSPEAKABLE WORSHIPPER

A young man came home to his beloved. He knocked on the door of her house and a voice from within asked: "Who's there? " He replied: "It's me." But the voice answered: "This house is not big enough for both of us." And the door remained closed.

Then the young man called out once more: "Dear, it's me; open up, I am here." But the door remained shut. Then the young lover withdrew into the forest and prayed and fasted in solitude. A year later, he returned and knocked once again at the door, and once more the voice asked: "Who's there? " And the young man then replied: "Dear, it's you." The door then opened so that he might go in.

— Jalaleddine Roumi

Adorable Father,
If only I had in my heart the one who
  worships you,
The Spirit whom you let enter in
  the world
So that a resounding song of souls
  might respond to you,

Adorable Father,
If I could without fail take hold
Of the grace on which human deeds
  depend,
Which holds them taut and brings them
  back to you,

Adorable Father,
If I had received the spirit of your Son,
As he was incarnate on earth,
So as to take on everything with passion
  and translate all into light,

Adorable Father,
I would sing your ineffable Trinity,
Not I, but your unspeakable Worshipper,
Not I, but ineffably our Lord,
Adorable Father!

> — Patrice de la Tour du Pin, *Une
> Somme de poésie*, t. 1.

Wake up, then, believer, and give careful heed to what is stated here, *"in my name"*: for in these words He does not say, "whatsoever ye shall ask" in any way; but, "in my name." How, then, is He called, who promised so great a blessing? Christ Jesus, of course: Christ means King, and Jesus means Saviour! ... By not doing what He sees to be contrary to our salvation, He manifests Himself the more fully as our Saviour. For the physician knows which of his patient's requests will be favorable, and which will be adverse, to his safety; and therefore yields not to his wishes when asking what is prejudicial, that he may effect his recovery.

> — St. Augustine, *Homilies on the Gospel
> of John*, 73, in *The Nicene and
> Post-Nicene Fathers of the Christian
> Church*, ed. Philip Schaff (Grand
> Rapids: Eerdmans, 1956), vol. VII.

It is true that this voice belongs to us and yet does not; that it is the voice of God's Spirit and yet is not. It is the voice of God's Spirit for if he did not inspire those words, we could neither pronounce nor even utter them. Nevertheless, it is not his voice for he does not feel either misery or fatigue; but these words are the cries of men in sorrow and pain. And so they are ours because they express our misery. At the same time, they are not ours since they are a gift from him.

— St. Augustine, *In Psalmos,* 144, 1

IN THE IMAGE OF HIS SON

And, looking upon them as he went,
Left them, by his glance alone,
clothed with beauty

... It must be known, then, that God looked at all things in this image of His Son alone, which was to give them their natural being, to communicate to them many natural gifts and graces and to make them finished and perfect, even as He says in Genesis, in these words: God saw all the things that He had made and they were very good [Genesis 1:31]. To behold them and find them very good was to make them very good in the Word, His Son. And not only did He communicate to them their being and their natural graces when He beheld them, as we have said, but also in this image of His Son alone He left them clothed with beauty, communicating to them supernatural being. This was when He became man, and thus exalted man in the beauty of God, and consequently exalted all the creatures in him, since in uniting Himself with man He united Himself with the nature of them all. Wherefore said the same Son of God: *Si ego exaltatus fuero a terra, omnia traham ad me ipsum* [John 12:32]. That is: I, if I be lifted up from the earth, will draw all things unto Me. And thus, in this lifting up of the Incarnation of His Son, and in the glory of His resurrection according to the flesh, not only did the Father beautify the creatures in part, but we can say that He left them all clothed with beauty and dignity.

> — St. John of the Cross, *Spiritual Canticle*, Stanza V, in *The Complete Works of Saint John of the Cross, op. cit.*, vol. II

The Shah of Persia one day gathered together all the artists of his kingdom and invited them to a contest. The problem was to reproduce the king's face. The Hindus came forth with marvelous colors, ochres and blues with which only they were familiar; then the Armenians came with a special kind of clay; next, the Egyptians appeared with unusual gouges and chissels, and very beautiful blocks of marble. Finally, the Greeks came, with but a small sachet of powder. Each delegation was locked for several weeks in the rooms of the palace. Then, on the appointed day, the King came and looked first at the marvelous works in ochre and blue of the Hindus, the models of the Armenians and the statues of the Egyptians, each more beautiful than the others. Finally, he came upon the Greeks, who had done only one thing: With their powder they had rubbed down and polished the marble wall where they were working, in such a way that when the king arrived, he saw only one thing — his own face, reflected on the wall.

It was, naturally, the Greeks who won the prize, since they realized that only the king could represent the king.

The same is also true of God and of Christ, as far as your life is concerned.   — Al Ghazzali

REMEMBER, O GLORIOUS FATHER

Majesty of God, behold the effects of un-speakable charity! Look at your dear child's mangled body. Examine these innocent hands from which flows sacred blood, and, once appeased, forgive the crimes which my hands have committed! Look at this defenseless side, pierced by a cruel sword; rejuvenate me in the flow of the holy fountain, which, I believe, has gushed forth from him. . .

Merciful Father, why do you not look at the head of this most beloved young son, at the drooping neck, at this unusual death and abandonment? O Gentle One, who produced us, consider the humanity of this beloved creature, and have pity on the weakness of all created flesh! His bare chest is white; his torn side is red; his dessicated insides burn! The royal face is livid! The arms are completely stiff; his sturdy legs are left hanging; and from his pierced feet flows a wave of sacred blood! Oh! look at your son's body, all torn, and then remember, O glorious Father, of what nature I am.

> — Jean de Fécamp, as cited by Daniel-Rops, *Mystiques de France* (Corrêa, 1958), p. 53

My God, please give me this *constant feeling of your presence*, your presence in and around me . . . and, at the same time, the frightened love one experiences in the presence of the one who is passionately loved, whereby a person stands before the beloved, unable to look at anything else, with the strong desire and complete deter-mination to do everything that pleases him, everything that is good for him, and also with the

great fear of doing, saying or thinking anything
that would displease or harm him... In you, by
you and for you. Amen

> — Charles de Foucauld, *Ecrits spirituels,
> op. cit.*, pp. 50-51

AT LAST YOUR LOVE

What moves me, O God, to love you
is not the heaven you have promised me:
it is not the awesome hell
which prompts me not to offend you.

It is you who prompt me, Lord:
it is seeing you nailed on the cross
  and insulted,
seeing your wounded body,
it is the insults you have received
  and your death.

Finally, it is your love,
so that I would love you
if there were no heaven,
And fear you
if there were no hell.

You need give me nothing
for me to love you,
for even if I would not hope for what I hope,
I would still love you as I love you now.

> — Anonymous, Spain (16th century)

Your face is the only fatherland for me.

> — St. Theresa of the Child Jesus

VI

THE WAY OF PERFECTION

*"Yea, I have loved thee with
an everlasting love: therefore
have I drawn thee, taking
pity on thee."*

—JEREMIAS 21:3

PRAYER NECESSARY FOR LIFE

HASAN Baçri one day saw a child holding a lighted torch.

"Where did you get that torch? " he asked.

The child then blew out the flame and said: "O Hasan! Tell me where it came from and then I will tell you where I got it."

God's will is like the light that is present in our lives: something very simple and yet, when we look at it, we can well ask: Where does it come from and where will it lead us? And yet, every day shows us that sanctity, or the road leading to God, has fixed points, constant landmarks. No matter who we are, sanctity will always require of us active cooperation with the power of God, and most of the time this will appear as some kind of purification.

Such cooperation takes place in the context of what is most vital in our lives, and more particularly as a result of the two basic forces in man: our activity and the desire to fulfill ourselves by means of it, and our heart and the desire to love and be loved. Where our strength lies, is where our purification and fulfillment will take place. Prayer is the possibility offered each day to cooperate with God. We should not, however, deceive ourselves; we hardly want our daily lives to take on the appearance of a "way of perfection." We are not asked to create our own strength in order to live for God; this strength comes from God. This is what we are reminded of by prayer.

Our task is to humbly prepare the terrain. But it would be erroneous for anyone to say that prayer acts by itself "provided that the Christian does not put any obstacle in the way," and to think that it is something negative, and hence easy. Such a person forgets that "not putting any obstacle in the way" actually requires a freely assumed commitment, a deliberate act on our part. He forgets that our very nature, because it is sinful and hence in a wounded state, is itself an obstacle. He forgets that when divine life tries to penetrate us through the medium of prayer, it encounters another law: the law of sin, "which circulates in my members" (Romans 7:23). Consequently, "not bringing forth any obstacle" is, in the final analysis, a privilege of sanctity. . . To arrive at that state, a man must work with all his strength to prepare the road, rework the land and offer to God when it is time for him to sow (an act that operates, as it were, like an autonomous life principle) a good, well-kept field (cf. the parable of the sower, Luke 8:4-9). The planting process has its own effects, but it does need the right kind of soil. It is an illusion to suppose that "not bringing forth any obstacle" would be easy since it involves nothing but receptivity; in truth, it is a work that is unusually difficult and painful.

HOPE AND PRAYER

Whether or not we wish, we cannot escape the thirst for happiness; we are made for it. Whether or not we wish, we cannot acquire it without human means. The Kingdom of God is not established outside of or beyond our lives, but each day as a result of the most insignificant acts. We actually enter into a collaboration with God when we begin our search for happiness.

But we must constantly be won over by God. God himself knows this. Thus, he makes our lives a long labor requiring patience in order to show us each day, a little more clearly, who he is and who we are. This labor has a name — the theological virtues — whereby God takes hold of our lives: with hope, our activity and desire for happiness; with charity, our love and our relationships with our fellowmen.

This is one of the most mysterious areas of our life, over which hope takes charge, and which we sense is most precious and also most fragile, the center and source of every impulse and every action. This part of our life is *our desire, this image of ourselves* which we still are not, and yet which we fashion and already possess within us, coming back to it constantly in our plans, dreams, regrets or fears. Even if we gradually overcome an immature attitude toward this image of ourselves and this "desire," and agree to put aside all sorts of illusions, this desire is still threatened throughout our entire life by a twofold danger: impatience and a tendency toward withdrawal.

First, *impatience*. Whether by temperament or a desire to be honest, we do not feel we are acting rightly toward God unless we are "doing something." God does not present himself right away. And yet, we do not have the time to wait. Our life is short. In view of our daily activity, professional work, family duties, we would like to "impinge upon Providence." We have often been told not to be satisfied with beautiful thoughts, and so we conclude that the "supernatural," like everything else, can be created, built, put together. Why, then, wait?

In addition, we are in the habit of doing almost nothing outside of our own plans, decisions and aspirations; thus we tend to seek out and find only ourselves, and, as a device of an obviously adolescent mind, to dominate our environment . . . and also Providence. As a result, we are astounded and confused when God's ways no longer seem to coincide with our own.

On the other hand, there is in us a *tendency toward withdrawal*. On behalf of the "spiritual," we more or less refrain from an honest examination of our daily tasks; for the sake of the "theological," we neglect moral effort. For the sake of an alleged "abandonment" to Providence, a so-called sense of the supernatural or principles describes as such, the "spiritual" life serves as an excuse for avoiding necessary struggles. We will reject real action and clear thinking in the belief that we will gain full possession of the spiritual life by a simple abdication of human responsibilities. How much phoniness could we not point to in our own lives, as the result of such an attitude!

Theology has long recognized these two attitudes — impatience or withdrawal, haste or scepticism regarding human action — namely, in Pelagianism and Quietism. Derived from the name of St. Augustine's adversary, Pelagius, Pelagianism placed too much emphasis on a misunderstood kind of freedom and made the acquisition of grace exclusively dependent on human effort, as if a person could return to God by sheer hard work. On the other hand, Quietism (from the Latin word meaning "rest") maintained that since everything came from God, it would be enough for man to seek rest in that love which surpasses him and makes virtuous effort unnecessary. These two tendencies appear regularly in our own lives as they have in the long history of the Church.

"God Makes Promises with His Creatures, but Holds only to Himself"

The problem is not whether we should use earthly means or not — whoever we are, we are forced to do so — but of believing that we can acquire, by our own efforts, the happiness that such means promise us.

Let us not think that this temptation arises only at special moments that are rare in our life, at the time of momentous decisions, such as when we are getting engaged or entering the novitiate... No, the smallest act involving choice presents us with this question: Is a person going to decide on doing something on behalf of a good that surpasses him, mindful of an external call or a light that he has received and is dominated by; or will he appoint himself as the sole principle of happiness and make himself God, his own god?

"God makes promises with his creatures, but holds only to himself," as Claudel remarked. Hope is sinful when it continually asks creatures to obtain by themselves what is promised them. This involves the subtle and awesome temptation to be one's own god, to become the sole arbiter of one's destiny, to feel need of no one, in a word to be certain that no form of dependence will prevent one from fulfilling himself.*

---

* Two examples can serve to illustrate this point: When Malraux stated the originality of the creative effort of the Greeks in his

Our prayer confronts these difficulties, especially when it is a question of the conduct of our *activity*, our actions, and *our need to be effective*. This does not mean, of course, that we shall be so crude as to pray only when we need to, for the purpose of some achievement or to avoid problems. Nevertheless, do we not often try to justify such times of retreat and silence, *first on the basis of a certain advantage?* And as it has been so often reported, we repeat to ourselves: "If I am not careful, I will fall prey to activism. To be myself, to be effective, to avoid wear and tear, I need this moment of recollection and silence; I must arrange some time for privacy. I will have to gather my resources together, regain strength, and bring about a spiritual re-charging. . ."

The Metamorphosis of the Gods, trans. Stuart Gilbert (Garden City, N. Y.: Doubleday & Company, Inc., 1960), pp. 59-60: "And what then arose for the first time (but not for the last) was a culture in which man, greatly daring, based his supreme values on his loftiest ideals and concentrated his efforts on all he could *do* to harmonize himself with them; not on what he ought to *be*, so as to attune himself to the eternal. 'Future generations,' Pericles proudly assured the Athenians 'will say of us: These men built up the most glorious and the happiest of cities. . .' For a dramatic change was coming over man's outlook on the scheme of things; he now was seeking within the hierarchy of his admirations and in the mysterious workings of what he regarded as the divine element in the universe, a power enabling him to do away with the sacred."

In the occasion when Camus was once being interviewed: "As I was getting off the train, a journalist asked me *whether I was going* to be converted. I answered: No. Nothing but the word, No. But I understand very well that faced with such an answer, a journalist feels the need to 'fill it out. . .' I am conscious of the sacred, of the mystery, which is in man, and I see no reason why I should not admit the emotion I feel regarding Christ and his teaching. Unfortunately, I fear that in certain milieux, in Europe especially, the admission of a lack of knowledge or the admission of a limit to man's knowledge, a respect for the sacred, appear to be signs of weakness. If these are weaknesses, I accept them completely. . ." (Interview of December 13, 1957, at the French Embassy in Stockholm).

What are we doing here if not measuring prayer and God's time by the advantages we hope to obtain? And so (despite the fact that in the end our life will be effective only if we do arrange these pauses, these moments of interior searching) we have adopted in practice one of the attitudes that mutilate prayer, that is the intense concern for a practical way of measuring things, for immediate effectiveness, the tendency to reduce everything to its "utilitarian" value. *In this way we appropriate our "desire" for ourselves, fashion it and falsify it according to our own ideas,* and therefore place ourselves in opposition to God. Thus, we offend against the virtue of hope, becoming incapable of understanding and foreseeing the mystery of God's ways. On the contrary, if our prayer is constant, it has the power to arouse in us and preserve the buoyancy of complete hope. It is only this kind of prayer that enables us to react positively to the attitude of God, and to understand his response to our desires and the way in which he satisfies our needs.

The Prodigal Son returned home out of necessity, since he had nothing left but acorns to eat. When he converts this distress into prayer, he changes everything, and this prevents him from making of his Father one "means" among others . . . that is, the last. And do not we ourselves need Christ and prayer, first of all, in order to succeed in our daily activities?

The Response of God – Certain, but Hidden

A number of parables demonstrate the nature of God's response to prayer. And just as the Apostles, caught in the storm, lose confidence before the amazingly serene and calm attitude of

Christ, we also are surprised by this response. The Gospels present it to us as unbelievably *certain,* unavoidable, assured of the result, free of any doubt about the outcome. The possibility of an eventual failure does not enter into consideration. The parable of the *sower* is pertinent here: thorns, rocks, a passerby can prevent the grain which has been sown from maturing, but there will always be a section of good earth to assure the harvest. Likewise, an enemy can spread *cockle* in the middle of a field, but he will not prevent the harvest. The *net* may contain fish of all kinds, there will still be enough to fill the vases. A *storm* can surprise a ship, but the latter, however, will arrive in the harbor.

In each of these parables, we become aware of the astonishing assurance of God; our Lord himself insists upon the certainty of the divine response. On other occasions, his whole attitude confirms this insistence: in Chapter 17 of St. John, as we have seen, he says: "I want. . .," and in Chapter 11: "I know that you always hear me" (John 11:42). What is the meaning of this insistence, if not that *by our prayer we begin to take possession of the almighty power of God*, not only through a promise which would very likely become true, due to the character and power of the one who made it, but through a promise that cannot fail to take place — *because it is all of a piece with absolute divine power*. It is nothing else but the strength of God, the very life of God at a moment in time, in history, in our own history. "God fashions us with our help."

The efficaciousness of prayer, as we have said, *does not depend first of all on us but on God.* St. Paul said, "So then there is question not of him who wills nor of him who runs, but of God showing mercy" (Romans 9:16). We now know that when we pray — provided we do not try to realize, at any price, our small plans and hopes — we become part of God's plan, the design he has decided to establish. We remind him once again of his promise to us. We intervene in the place he has left open for our intervention, and thus we are free to regain what we would have otherwise lost.

For Thirty Years I Searched for God

Here we become aware of the complete conversion, the about-face, that our attitude and imagination must make, as far as hope is concerned.

It is not we who wait for God, and draw his attention, but it is God who awaits us. It is not we who are anxious to see him realize our desires, but it is he, who wishes to enter into our plans and to invest us with his own strength. *And in prayer it is he who anticipates us, giving* us an opportunity to work for and with him, in the absolute certainty of success. "For thirty years I searched for God, and at the end I saw that it was he who was waiting for me."

This is the first response of God, the secret of our hope, and what should be the foundation of our certitude.

In this connection, it seems that too often we believe that the essential element in hope ("its formal object," as we say) is the desire to possess happiness and to possess God. Yet the essential note of hope is not primarily the desire for beatitude, but the assurance that God comes to our aid. Here theology does nothing but translate in an admirable way the lesson of the Bible.

We are in the habit of feeling that the movement of hope goes this way: I desire infinite, divine happiness; therefore, I shall ask God to help me. But it is the reverse that is true. The proper movement of Christian hope is this: (1) I put my trust in God; (2) in order that he might give himself to me. God offers himself as an "auxiliary," an aid, and the reason for this is that the good promised is God himself, who is infinite. But this we do not discover until after we have accepted the "Alliance" with God and put ourselves in his hands.

✓ This reversal, this about-face, to which the Bible invites us, has not been sufficiently described. It is not a matter of one deed, one isolated case. It is a constant occurrence. When God speaks to man, he first of all proposes to him his Alliance, offers him his aid and assistance. It is really himself that he is proposing. *But he does this only after revealing the "reason for" this aid.* The Alliance is the first thing proposed, and if I accept it I put myself in his hands in an absolute way. Then will I understand the reason for this proposition, the goal toward which the Alliance will lead me. It is the Alliance that is first of all revealed to me, but for the purpose of bringing me, little by little, to desire the vision, the Kingdom.

How clear this is in the life of each witness in the Bible! The call and alliance come first, then the promise and the Kingdom: "I shall be with you"; then, "I shall be your reward." "Do not be afraid, Abraham, I am your shield. Your reward shall be very great" (Genesis 15:1). But Abraham learns only gradually what this reward will be. If he puts his trust completely in God, even to the point of giving him his only son, he will understand the reason why God delays: if God proposes himself slowly, if he takes his time in answering Abraham's prayer (cf. the episode of Sodom and Gomorrha, Genesis 18), it is because the reward will be "very great." The sin of Christians will be to ask God to help them obtain only limited goals. If God himself offers to help us, in the last analysis it is only for the purpose of giving himself . . . and not simply to assure some particular result (for example, at the Annunciation: "The Lord be with you" — "You will conceive a son, he will be great and will be called Son of the Most High"). Hope that longs for a miracle is not virtuous insofar as it does not go to the root of divine aid and assistance; it still waits for "something," even if this something is extraordinary. That is why we cannot begrudge God if he dealys his response. . . In this way, he leads us to discovering how far he wants to lead us, by means of this help.

The entire history of God's People in the Old Testament is constantly marked by the "delays" of God. Insofar as this history has the value of a law, we should presume that the pattern will not be different for us: God makes us wait for him when we pray. The Bible is filled with instances where it seems that God should not change his mind (see, among others: Genesis 18, Abraham before Sodom; II Samuel 12:15, ff., David; II Kings 20; Isaiah 18, Ezechiel, etc.) or where he has no desire that his response should be as rapid as man would like. (See Exodus 32-33, Moses; the entire book of Job; II Samuel 12-18, the entire history of David after the adultery up to the death of Absalom.) It would be blasphemous to imagine God as a tyrant who would procrastinate out of a sense of pleasure, as if he needed such stratagems to assert himself. . . .

The More Obscure, the More Certain

The certitude of the divine response is real only insofar as it surpasses us. For it is absolute and guaranteed only because it is divine, and hence disproportionate to our own means of action. This is why, however paradoxical it may appear, *the more obscure, baffling, hidden it is, the more certain it is.* This is the second aspect of God's response as seen in the parables: the efficaciousness of prayer is transcendent. This efficacy is also hidden. "Why are you fearful, O you of little faith? " (Matthew 8:26). At the most violent point in a storm, we know neither how or when the soul will be pacified. And a man will not discover the results of a harvest or a catch of fish — despite the cockle — until the master arrives. And he who has planted the mustard seed, will find out only in the end whether it can produce a tree: ". . . As though a man should cast seed into the earth, then sleep and rise, night and day, and the seed should sprout and grow without his knowing it" (Mark 4:27). Likewise for the leaven, which would lose all its strength if it were not hidden.

So it is in our life: for the moment, we are still in the night, just before dawn, like men on watch. "Upon your walls, O Jerusalem, I have stationed watchmen; never, by day or by night, shall they be silent. O you who are to remind the Lord, take no rest and give no rest to him, until he re-establishes Jerusalem and makes of it the pride of the earth" (Isaiah 62:6-7). "Watch, therefore, for you do not know at what hour your Lord is to come" (Matthew 24:42). And like a watchman, a sentinel at an outpost, we see only the sector we are guarding, nothing farther on. Victory is certain, but it is never perceived by

those who are fighting. It is enough for them to
carry on the fight and hold their position, however uncertain and insignificant it may be. In our
life, we see only the one side of events. But with
God's help we can trace out, in prayer, the plan
he has selected for us.

And we find this perplexing because he has the
time to do so, but more so because he answers
our requests and *gives much more according to
his own kindness than according to the nature of
our requests, so much so that often in receiving
his gifts we do not recognize the precise thing we
had sought.* "Now, to him who is able to
accomplish all things in a measure far beyond
what we ask or conceive, in keeping with the
power that is at work in us — to him be glory in
the Church and in Christ Jesus down through all
the ages of time without end. Amen! "
(Ephesians 3:20-21).

It is fortunate that our prayer is not limited to
the efficaciousness we too often desire! For its
measure of achievement would only be as meager
as our own limited selves. Consider the Prodigal
Son: What does he want? To become a servant.
That would suffice for him. How is his request
answered? Superabundantly — he becomes a son
again and with choice rank. The old woman
Anna, wife of Samuel, would like a child, even
agreeing to dedicate it to God. And God makes
this child one of the greatest leaders of the
Jewish people. The manna in the desert, the
multiplication of the loaves, and the miraculous
catch of fish: everywhere God responds "above
and beyond." And this is what first disturbs us:
because God empties himself to an infinite
degree.

Because You Were a Man of Desire

How does this divine attitude affect our prayer? Before the mystery and transcendence of God's response, should we renounce all personal concerns, divest ourselves of all human interests and desires and abandon ourselves to quietism? No, because when God comes to Daniel, it is to tell him that, "I have come to you because you were a man of desire" (Daniel 9:23). It is not a matter of destroying and annihilating our life plan, but of *making it real.*

If true prayer discloses the real reason for our hope, and shows us that it is important for us that *God* be efficacious, we can understand how it preserves the human root of our desire and hope, and, what is more, makes it possible and real. Not only does it preserve God in us it also preserves the man.

This is one of the first effects of prayer. And one of the most beautiful privileges of its efficaciousness is to make real the desire we express in it. In every prayer there is a kind of shock effect in return. Only God has the power to make every request and every invocation addressed to him penetrate completely the desire of the one expressing it; to make this desire "be," to make it "real." Thus, in a certain sense, every prayer is already answered, for it has given the best part of ourselves an opportunity to exist.

Not only does prayer give our desire the chance to exist, but — and this is its second duty as to hope — it modifies it and makes it more true. Prayer means accepting this conversion, this about-face, of ourselves for the sake of Another.

Making our desire real does not mean it will not change. Herein lies the power of prayer: "Amazing how my ideas change when I pray over

them" (Bernanos). Scripture has left us examples
of such changes. St. Peter and St. Paul are
brought to modifying some very important
decisions for the Church (Acts 10: 9ff.; 16:3;
21:17ff). St. Paul will not be freed of his goad,
that thorn in his flesh, despite his repeated
requests (II Corinthians 12:7-9) but in the
meantime he begins to understand the reason for
this and even makes his weakness serve the glory
of God. God did not answer his prayer according
to the terms of his original request, but as a
result of his changed viewpoint St. Paul gains a
new understanding of the special way in which
God looks upon his life. God is indeed a Father,
but parents would be wrong if they satisfied all
the requests of their children, heeded their first
desire, which is often nothing else but pure
whim. St. Augustine said: "We have the right to
ask for everything we have the right to desire."
But we do not have the "right" to any and all
desire. On the other hand, whatever is good for
us, we have more than a right — indeed, a duty —
to ask for it. And so, in our prayers, Christ does
not suppress but rather rectifies our desires, for
example, in the case of the mother of the sons of
Zebedee: "You do not know what you are asking
for" (Mark 10:35ff.). And yet it is important to
draw closer and closer to God. Thus, God keeps
watch over our desire — sometimes in spite of
ourselves — and protects us from temptations and
perversions of this desire.

Christ does not advise the mother of Zebedee's
sons to ask for nothing, but induces her to ask
for something else.

Thus, the purpose of prayer is perhaps less to
obtain what we ask than to *Become someone
else*. We should go further and say that asking
something from God transforms us, little by

little, into people capable of sometimes doing without what they ask for.

Let us not attempt to state too quickly and *a priori* the laws regarding the transformation of our desires and the orientation of our lives. It will be different for each person. The stages will be as diverse as the movement of a river, where everything depends so much on the territory traversed. On each man's journey, there will be meanderings, those times when we do not seem to be moving ahead, and also huge gaps and the call of the estuary. Let us not be surprised that there are "ages" in the life of prayer as there are in the life of man. Here and there, the interplay between desire and a sense of the real and the situation at hand that varies according to the past and future, shape the major parts of a man's life, just as graces and temptations do. But whatever his age, true prayer will always be effective in preserving the infinite that man desires and the image he has of a God who calls him, by protecting him against the illusion of false haste and against a retreat occasioned by pessimism and a feeling of abandonment.

Now we understand why God seems to delay: not in order to test us arbitrarily, but to compel our desire to become more intense and to become truly like his. While we judge such delays with our eyes and according to our defeats, God judges them according to reality.

This is why only he is effective. The education he gives, his pedagogy, is not an unjustifiable sport, which is gratuitous and of no value. If God takes his time, he does so for our sake. Because of the unusually delicate nature of his love, he does not want to effect our happiness without us, but wants to produce it from within, to make us work at it and to give it to us only after exhausting the possibilities of our waiting. "God fashions us with our help." Because of love, God cannot fail to take into account that desire which he placed in us to serve as an aid to his giving.

The purpose of prayer is to bring this desire, which leaves a man restless and disturbed, to becoming a feeling of hope, guaranteed not like a machine, with its momentary usefulness, but by an infinite effectiveness since it comes from God himself.

Doing without God and being sufficient unto ourselves, or else accepting the infinite — this is the dialectic of hope, happiness and prayer. "Man's desire has no remedy" (St. Theresa of Avila). "What distinguishes man is that he can solve his own problems and knows it" (Karl Marx). Whoever we are, we must decide between these two options.

Read the following passages from the Gospel:

(1) *The parables of waiting:* Matthew 25:6ff.; Mark 13:35ff.; Matthew 24:43-50.

(2) *The parables of the coming of the Kingdom and the certitude of Christ:* John 17:24 and 11:42; Matthew 13:1-51.

(3) *The meaning of God's delays:* II Peter 3:8-9; Judith 8:10-27 and 9:5-6; Genesis 18 (Abraham), II Samuel 12:15ff. (David); Isaiah 38 (Ezechiel); II Corinthians 12:7-9 (St. Paul).

(4) *The conversion necessary in order to have one's requests heard:* dependence on God (Mark 14:39; Luke 8:43; John 5:8; Matthew 15:22; etc.). For the opposite view, see Mark 9:23, Matthew 20:20, etc.

PRAYER OR CHARITY?

It takes time to put aside our illusions about charity. Of course, we are in agreement with the Gospels when they give priority to love over all other Christian duties. As soon as people talk about charity and love, we are *a priori* in agreement.

But we sometimes show little courage in really acting out our life of charity, and in purifying it. How often does it not simply reflect our natural feelings, our need for an extended paternity or maternity! Everything can be used to justify our egotism and self-seeking under the guise of charity: apostolate, commitment, activity... Amid all this, it is so easy to seek out and find ourselves.

Fortunately, at certain times in our life, a conflict between charity and prayer almost always arises. Quite simply, because of the lack of time.

On the one hand, the Gospels state as the first great law of prayer the obligation to pray unceasingly, continually, on all occasions, as we have already seen. The passages in the New Testament are unanimous on this point, as later on the spiritual masters of the Church will be. All of our life can become subject matter for prayer. A person can no more do away with God than he can with himself.

On the other hand, we believe in the primacy of charity. We are convinced of this primacy and its urgency, and with the passing of time this conviction increases within us, becomes more pressing — and rightly so. And to such an extent that at moments of great distress our conscience bothers us, and we feel guilty. And yet, if someone should then stress the importance of prayer, we may well answer: "Why waste our time and strength in prayer when we could do something more useful? " Or else, when confronted by the difficulty and effort required to pray daily, it seems that our dedication and suffering ought to suffice: "In my case, my prayer is my work."

We know how serious this tension between prayer and charity has been in the history of the Church ("contemplative" life vs. "active" life, etc.), as well as in the life of each human being, and how regularly the problem of the formal object of charity is examined in theology. Claudel put it this way: "The temptation facing modern man is to show that people do not need God in order to do good."

A Different Kind of Love

It is obvious that maintaining a balance here is not easy. In every way of life, the difficulty arises in one form or another: To whom should priority be given, to God or other men? How is this problem solved in our own life?

"It is love alone that counts," says St. Theresa of Lisieux in repeating the Gospels. We are sensitive to such statements. They immediately win secret approbation in our heart. And we like to tell ourselves over and over again that this is the essence of Christianity, its center, and that it is radically different from the lofty heights of pseudo-mysticism. "Blessed are the meek, the mild, the merciful. . . You will be judged according to your life." All such statements, since they are concrete, speak to us directly.

And we are right: our conviction will undoubtedly remain always on this side of the state-

ments of the Gospel and the example of the
Apostles. For the latter also, and their unanimity
is impressive, there is no doubt: in the hierarchy
of Christian deeds, the summit is love. "Thou
shalt not commit adultery. Thou shalt not kill.
Thou shalt not steal. Thou shalt not covet; and if
there is any other commandment, it is summed
up in this saying, Thou shalt love thy neighbor as
thyself. Love does no evil to a neighbor. Love
therefore is the fulfillment of the Law" (Romans
13:9-10). "Therefore all that you wish men to do
to you, even so do you also to them; for this is
the Law and the Prophets" (Matthew 7:12). "He
who does not love does not know God; for God
is love" (I John 4:8 and John 4:29 and 13:35).
"But above all these things have charity, which is
the bond of perfection" (Colossians 3:14).

To understand this primacy of love in the life
of Christians, and not reduce it to a simple,
natural yearning for solidarity, it is perhaps
necessary to discover the difficulty implied and
to appreciate the fact that it involves going
beyond one's limitations.

"It is love alone that counts." We are convinced of this and yet how easily we maintain
our illusions about this love! Exercising by
instinct a certain strictness as to other failings,
how indulgently we often judge our shortcomings
in the area of charity (consider our lack of
seriousness regarding sinful remarks or the refusal
to participate in community life)! But if we are
strict regarding weakness or deviations — senti-
mental or otherwise — in our prayer life, what a
lack of lucidity we show regarding those of our
life of charity, of commitment, in other words,
of our apostolate.

It is not unusual if charity should involve other
difficulties than the simple struggle against the

natural egotism of man. (We remember the statement of Professor de Greeff: "He who claims to be fighting for freedom but who does not also fight for the freedom of his enemy, is not fighting for *freedom* but for *his own* freedom.")

We are fortunate if courage in a task we have not chosen, constancy in a long trial, the ingratitude and malice of the recipients of our commitment, and perhaps desertion, jealousy and betrayal allow us to discover the Christian meaning of charity, namely, that *it is a different kind of love.*

Actually, we are not sufficiently convinced of the originality of this "Christian" love and too often unaware of its unbelievable difficulty.

Briefly, let us recall its main laws. There are two, which are related to two important passages: Luke 10, the parable of the Good Samaritan; John 13, the last discourse of Christ. Everything else that can be said about this matter is included in these passages.

*Having a Neighbor, or
Making Oneself Neighborly?*

The parable of the Good Samaritan converges on the final reversal of the question that opened the debate. At the beginning, a doctor of the Law asks: "Who is my neighbor? " At the end, our Lord, reversing the question, asks: "Which of these three proved himself neighbor to him who fell among the robbers? "

The first golden rule of Christian charity is to make oneself neighborly. "Who proved himself to be neighbor to the wounded man on the road? " This does not merely involve asking myself who is my neighbor, who belongs to my group, my "relations," my class — this is the thinking of the

Old Testament. Jesus said — and this is the New Testament: if someone is not neighborly toward you (for the Samaritan, this meant an enemy), it is up to you to approach him and be neighborly toward him, and if there is no reason for acting so, you should create one. This does not merely mean not "failing" in charity: "Father, I did harm to no one"; but having a neighbor, that is making oneself, in a positive way, neighborly. Of whom? of whoever is on my path or is in need. And if his suffering is greater than mine, this will mean giving preference to his suffering over mine. This is part of the unlimited range of the second commandment, which is similar to the first.

As Christ Loved Us

How make myself neighborly? What is the second law of charity? The answer is clear: "Love one another as I have loved you" (John 13:34). "Even as the Lord has forgiven you, so also do you forgive" (Colossians 3:13). Love will be Christian and will attain true charity only insofar as it will conform to the love of Christ, and will be that of Christ. All of Jesus' acts are permeated with the laws of such conformity. All his life reveals to us how he loved.

1. His love is, first of all, a love that gives, that is pure gift. He comes to us without demands. He does not condemn, he does not begin by judging. Although we have offended him, he is the one who comes to propose reconciliation. "His love consists of this: it is not we who loved God, he loved us. . . He loved us first" (John 4:10-19). As to the Samaritan woman, the widow of Naim, Zacheus, the paralytic at Capharnaum, the multiplication of the loaves of bread,

it is always he who starts things off, he who takes the first steps. He loves as a *pure gift*, for the sake of nothing; he *gives* by taking the *initiative, gratuitously*. Note how this love is the opposite of our usual attitude. We are always soothed by this immense illusion: the ready belief that we are very attentive, affectionate, capable of generosity, eager to love, and that "if things don't work out" the fault is someone else's because they are not lovable. To relieve ourselves of our failures and inadequacies, we then accuse their defects, their mediocrity. Our Lord acts in just the opposite way. He makes others better by loving them. Not only does he not accuse their mediocrity, although it is his full right to do so — infinitely more than we could — but he takes up their defense and gives his heart, his time, his trust.

Against Simon the Pharisee, Judas and Martha, he defends Mary Magdalene, as he defended the Samaritan woman and Zacheus against public opinion or his Apostles. He knew that if such people were weak, small, mediocre, it is precisely because they lacked the love to grow and because others did not love them enough.

What does our Lord do? He calls forth, arouses, renews the best part in man, the part that is good and filled with hope and is always hidden in each and every person. Because Christ loves, and shows his love in creating new and good things — and for no ulterior motive — everybody who meets him once again begins to believe, to have trust in God and in themselves. His love is above all a pure, gratuitous gift, and in this way he manifests the Father and shows us that the first step in love is to be a source of life, and that only he who loves shares in the life of God. "Experience has shown me *too late* that we cannot judge people by their vices, but on the contrary by what they hold intact and pure, by the childlike qualities that remain in them, however deeply one must search for them" (George Bernanos, *Lettre aux Anglais*, p. 92).

2. Not only does Christ give, but he does so *by making himself smaller than we are:* at Christmas an infant, at the Agony a beggar, and before the Samaritan woman, Zacheus and Mary Magdalene, with the washing of the feet. At every moment, Christ puts himself on a lower level than those he loves, accepts the fact that he needs them, not for the sake of some strategy or clever calculation, but to evoke in such people the best part of their being — their heart, their generosity — in order to make them capable of giving in their turn.

3. This love that gives to others by making itself smaller, goes so far as giving up life and dying on the Cross. "God so loved the world that he gave his only-begotten Son..." (John 3:16). "Greater love than this no one has, that one lay down his life for his friends" (John 15:13). He did not love us "as some kind of joke," but because he was himself, and as if we deserved his life. This is the real meaning of "to love my neighbor as myself."

But that's impossible, you will say. Yes, for man alone, and in his lucid moments man recognizes that it is impossible. Between human love, human solidarity, however strong it may be, and charity there is not only a difference of degree, of intensity, but a *difference of nature*. Charity is a completely different kind of love. "I give you a *new* commandment." Christ commands us to love as he himself loves, as God loves. Charity is a love that comes from above. "Bear one another's burdens, and so you will fulfill the law of Christ" (Galatians 6:2). A burden that is not heavy is not a burden. And actually bearing the burden of others is impossible for a man who is already aware of his own problems. Yes, a new love is necessary, one that comes from God.

"It is love alone that counts," but St. Teresa added: "To love as you love me, I must borrow your kind of love, for only then will I find peace." This is the novel feature of the commandment: to love with the very love of God. What is new in the New Testament, is not that God asks us to love (this was already the Law of the Old Testament), but that he asks us to love with the same love he has for himself and for everything he does. No one else had ever said that we can share in the divine fecundity itself, that God will give us what we need to love him, and to love others in the way that he himself loves.

This explains the strange equivalence established by our Lord between what is done to others, "to the little ones," and what is done to God. One enters into relationships with other men, and it is God himself who responds. Almost as if by some law of the mysterious reciprocity of relationships God waited for us to be witnesses and representatives of his own paternity.

And this is where charity and prayer converge: far from opposing each other, they evoke each other and mutually save one another.

Charity Impossible without Prayer —
Prayer Impossible without Charity

All charity is founded upon prayer. For how can

a person claim to love his brother "as God loves him," "for the love of God," if he does not know what this love is and what it implies. Or if it is only a question of ideas, very beautiful perhaps, but with nothing more behind them, if one has not given existence to or become conscious of the concrete meaning of God's love? A person does not love, and is not loved, by proxy. Moreover, a person loves and is loved only in the present. Love has no existence in the past. Its relationship to time is unlike that of thought. The remembrance of love is not love. (Just as in the case of illness: I can recall that I was sick, but I do not recall the sickness itself, unless by falling sick again. . .)

This is why prayer must be present when an act of charity is performed. To really love, I must find out how I am loved, and this must actually be experienced. To love as God loves, presupposes that a person has been affected by this love and has experienced its attraction and its piercing strength. Thus, knowing how one is loved and actually loving someone become part of the one act: the second commandment is "like" the first. Without prayer, without the perpetual presence within us, at least in memory, of the divine origin of true fraternal charity, a person can only live out a caricatured version of charity.

Thus, *by revealing how Christ, God, have loved us, prayer will establish the basis for charity.* First, by *meditation on the Gospels.* "If thou didst know the gift of God" (John 4:10) — no one has ever known this in a concrete way or seen its effect in the present. No one has ever completely grasped everything Christ has done for us, and the fact "that he did not love us as some kind of joke." Thus, prayer nourishes in me a vivid recollection of what God has done and of the price he paid for my salvation. Recalling God — at the present moment — is the essence of prayer, its first movement. It is a new reminder of what the redemption of my life actually cost.

The purpose of Scripture, meditated upon prayer, is to make clear the reality of this divine love for each of us, and to make it clear in a concrete way by the acts of our Lord, which are in effect vivid parables of God's mercy and expressions of his permanent laws. "As I have loved you. . ." Only when we have discovered the various stages of this love, although gradually and at least in our desire, can someone else to some extent depend on us as he depends on the love of God.

"Bear one another's burdens, and so you will fulfill the law of Christ (Galatians 6:2). Let us not be mistaken: being patient, mild, willing to receive people and listen to them, all conditions of true charity, are impossible if day after day we do not discover the patience, forbearance and tenderness of God for us. . .

Loving one's neighbor "for the love of God" must be understood in a second, though no less real, sense: in order that he also might love God. The Church is the community of the saints and of those moving toward Beatitude. My prayer, therefore, will be part of the Church insofar as it assumes responsibility for the community of saints, is productive of communion and yearns for the Spirit of charity to be the link that truly unites all Christians.

This is the *object of prayer*, although it is not, however, visible to everyone. To avoid misunderstandings, it can never be stressed enough how much of a mystery true charity is. We must believe in it, for it is an article of faith. Men are not called to unite in just any kind of community, but in the relationship that unites the Father and the Son. *It is from this mysterious, divine union that charity arises.* The Spirit of Love is not just any kind of "link"; it unites us to God, by allowing us to share in the intimacy of the Father and Son, and unites us to one another — inevitably — in this same image. This is why we do not see the ultimate goal of love, when it is directed toward our neighbor; we do, however, believe in it. I love my neighbor in the same relationship that exists between him and his God, his Father and my Father.

Knowing through faith, then, what is meant by the statement "God loves," I am able to discover what is worthy of God in the world, and to realize that man — every man — is a sacred being, that my neighbor's heart was born, like mine, from the same love of the Father, that he yearns for God in the same divinely originated way, and that I am called to love him in the same way that God loves me and I love him. Just as faith is transmitted to me by intermediaries and signs that I cannot do without, and which I must pass beyond, so the love of God passes through my neighbor and returns to God through him. God comes down to me through my brother so that I might come to God by loving him. This takes place by means of prayer, which alone places charity under the sign of the Spirit and preserves it against all its false and tempting imitations, such as those of solidarity or collective pride, however ecclesiastical they may be.

All Those You Command Me to Love

Charity is impossible without prayer, strenuous prayer, but the purpose of prayer is derived from charity; if it is not, it is nothing but a lie. Every prayer is summed up in the agreement of two wills: "Thy will be done, thy kingdom come. . ." Praying means becoming a disciple of Jesus, of him who is loved by the Father. But how can we recognize such disciples? "By this will all men know that you are my disciples, if you have love for one another" (John 13:35). Praying means reuniting oneself to Christ, sharing his will. And what is his will? "A new commandment I give you, that you love one another" (John 13:3). "Holy Father, keep in thy name those whom thou hast given me, that they may be one even as we are" (John 17:11). "Thy will be done," and St. Teresa added, "Your will is to love in and through me all those whom you command me to love."

"Thy will be done": our prayer, our "practice," will be judged according to our charity, and our charity will be judged by our fellowmen. An anecdote taken from Yafii, a Mohammedan mystic, will suffice to illustrate this:

A friend of Ibn-Al-Kabchi one day asked him to show him Khidr, the mysterious personage who sometimes reveals himself to mystics during a state of ecstasy.

"I will show him to you on Friday, God willing," said Ibn-Al-Kabchi.

Very happy, the man then went and distributed an entire silo of wheat to the poor — for he was a rich man — and on the same day he began to pray.

Then someone knocked at his door. The servant went to see who it was and came back to report it was a beggar.

"Tell him to come back after my prayer," answered the rich man.

The day passed without any further incident. The next day he complained to his friend:

"I did not see Khidr, as you promised me."

"On the contrary; he was the beggar whom you told to return later."

Saying to a poor man, "I will give you something tomorrow," is the same as chasing God away. It is not surprising that the great New Testament text (the First Epistle of St. John) on God-as-Love is also the one that is most emphatic about the concrete requirements of charity. And who can claim that he observes all the rules in this connection?

"If anyone says, 'I love God,' and hates his brother, he is a liar. For how can he who does not love his brother, whom he sees, love God, whom he does not see? " (I John 4:29).

It is said that at the end of the nineteenth century John Bosco had to spend a short time in Paris. He went to the rectory of a large church, in the center of Paris. Seeing this Italian priest, who was perhaps of poor appearance and no doubt with hesitant French, the parish priest gave him a room in an attic on the sixth floor. Several years later, the same priest, questioned in Rome about Don Bosco during the canonization process, made this naive as well as awesome remark: "Well, of course, if we had known he was a saint, we wouldn't have put him on the sixth floor! "

In this regard, we need only read once again Chapter 25 of St. Matthew, which contains the great scene of the very last judgment of men and nations. "Lord, when did we see thee hungry . . . or thirsty . . . or a stranger? . . . Amen I say to you, as long as you did it for one of these, the least of my brethren, you did it for me." "Well, of course, if we had known he was a saint. . ." It was Christ himself.

Prayer or charity? Note the question as it is put: it can be absolutely false. It is no longer related to the Old Testament. Charity involves sharing part of God's heart and discovering, through my prayer, the infinite dimensions of his love. Prayer means saying this: thy will be done, and therefore bring to reality, through my actions, thy will of love, pardon and mercy. Henceforth, there will be but one commandment, that which, because it concerns the most precious part of God's life — his love — will serve to judge us. And it will judge us not on the basis of some rare skill, but on the basis of a salvation whose measure is close at hand: my fellowman, my neighbor. As if the marvelous novelty of the Gospels was in asking us to have henceforth for others the attitude we have for God, and for God the one he has for us. Thus, it is, indeed, love alone that counts. As if the only way for us to affirm that we have a Father in heaven, is to show that we really do have brothers, while realizing that one cannot be a brother to all, a "universal brother," unless each day as a result of prayer, we live, on the certainty that we are all loved by the same Father.

Read once again the following passages of the Gospels:

(1) *The primacy of charity:* Romans 13:9-10; Matthew 7:12; John 13:35; I John 4:8, 20; Colossians 3:13-14.

(2) *The newness of this commandment:* John 13:34; Colossians 3:13; Galatians 6:2; I John 3:16; John 15:13.

(3) *Prayer and charity. Knowing God means having the same Spirit as he, thus the same attitude as he regarding our fellowmen:* I John 4:7-8; Osee 4:1 and 6:6; Isaiah 57 and 58; Jerome 9:23 and 22:13-17; Malachia 3:4-5; Matthew 25; I John 4:21.

READINGS

SEARCHING FOR HIM
WHO SEARCHES AFTER US

I am not looking for peace but the face of Him who gives the peace I ask for in prayer.

We think it is we who are searching after God, whereas it is really we who are being sought. Our search is the result of the discomfit in us caused by the secret, unceasing, gratuitous and tenacious quest for a kind of mercy about which we know very little. The presence of such mercy is perhaps made clear to our heart only when we are plunged in a confusion whose source is unknown to us. We then endeavor to locate this source without knowing what is happening to us, nor what we desire or why, nor even whether we desire it. When the light finally dawns and we realize what we are lacking, we then think of looking for God, at the very moment when he is finally reaching us, touching us, holding on to us.

THE HOUND OF HEAVEN

I fled Him, down the nights and
    down the days;
 I fled Him, down the arches of the years;
I fled Him, down the labyrinthine ways
  Of my own mind; and in the mist of tears
I hid from Him, and under running laughter.
    Up vistaed hopes I sped;
    And shot, precipitated,
Adown Titanic glooms of chasmèd fears,
  From those strong Feet that followed,
    followed after.
    But with unhurrying chase,
    And unperturbèd pace,
  Deliberate speed, majestic instancy,
    They beat — and a Voice beat
    More instant than the Feet —
"All things betray thee, who betrayest Me."

    I pleaded, outlaw-wise,
By many a hearted casement, curtained red,
 Trellised with intertwining charities
(For, though I knew His love Who followèd,
    Yet was I sore adread
Lest, having Him, I must have naught
    beside);
But, if one little casement parted wide,
  The gust of His approach would clash it to:
  Fear wist not to evade, as Love wist
    to pursue.
Across the margent of the world I fled,
  And troubled the gold gateways of
    the stars,
  Smiting for shelter on their clangèd bars;

Fretted to dulcet jars
And silvern chatter the pale ports o'
     the moon,
I said to Dawn: Be sudden — to Eve:
     Be soon;
  With thy young skiey blossoms heap
     me over
     From this tremendous Lover —
Float thy vague veil about me, lest He see!
  I tempted all His servitors, but to find
My own betrayal in their constancy,
In faith to Him their fickleness to me,
  Their traitorous trueness, and
     their loyal deceit.
To all swift things for swiftness did I sue;
  Clung to the whistling mane of every wind.
     But whether they swept, smoothly fleet,
  The long savannahs of the blue;
     Or whether, Thunder-driven,
     They clanged his chariot 'thwart a heaven,
Plashy with flying lightings round the
     spurn o' their feet: —
Fear wist not to evade as Love wist to
     pursue.
     Still with unhurrying chase,
     And unperturbed pace,
  Deliberate speed, majestic instancy,
     Came on the following Feet,
     And a Voice above their beat —
"Naught shelters thee, who wilt not
     shelter Me."

I sought no more that after which I strayed
     In face of man or maid;
But still within the little children's eyes
     Seems something, something that replies,
They at least are for me, surely for me!

I turned me to them very wistfully;
But just as their young eyes grew
    sudden fair
  With dawning answers there,
Their angel plucked them from me by
    the hair.
"Come then, ye other children, Nature's
  — share
With me" (said I) "your delicate fellowship;
  Let me greet you lip to lip,
  Let me twine with you caresses,
    Wantoning
  With our Lady-Mother's vagrant tresses,
    Banqueting
  With her in her wind-walled palace,
  Underneath her azured dais,
  Quaffing, as your taintless way is,
    From a chalice
Lucent-weeping out of the dayspring."
    So it was done:
I in their delicate fellowship was one —
Drew the bolt of Nature's secrecies.
  I knew all the swift importings
  On the willful face of skies;
  I knew how the clouds arise
  Spumèd of the wild sea-snortings;
    All that's born or dies
  Rose and drooped with; made them shapers
Of mine own moods, or wailful or divine;
  With them joyed and was bereaven.
  I was heavy with the even,
  When she lit her glimmering tapers
  Round the day's dead sanctities.
  I laughed in the morning's eyes.
I triumphed and I saddened with all weather,
    Heaven and I wept together,
  And its sweet tears were salt with mortal
    mine;

Nigh and nigh draws the chase,
  With unperturbèd pace,
Deliberate speed, majestic instancy;
  And past those noisèd Feet
  A Voice comes yet more fleet —
"Lo! naught contents thee, who
    content'st not Me."

Naked I wait Thy love's uplifted stroke!
My harness piece by piece Thou hast hewn
    from me,
  And smitten me to me knee;
  I am defenseless utterly.
  I slept, methinks, and woke,
And, slowly gazing, find me stripped
    in sleep.
In the rash lustihead of my young powers,
  I shook the pillaring hours
And pulled my life upon me;
    grimed with smears,
I stand amid the dust o' the
    mounded years —
My mangled youth lies dead beneath
    the heap.
  Ah! is Thy love indeed
A weed, albeit an amaranthine weed,
Suffering no flowers except its
    own to mount?
  Ah! must —
  Designer infinite! —
Ah! must Thou char the wood ere Thou
    canst limn with it?
My freshness spent its wavering shower
    i' the dust;
And now my heart is as a broken fount,
Wherein tear-drippings stagnate,
    spilt down ever

From the dank thoughts that shiver
Upon the sighful branches of my mind.
  Such is; what is to be?
The pulp so bitter, how shall taste the rind?
I dimly guess what Time in mists confounds;
Yet ever and anon a trumpet sounds
His name I know, and what his
    trumpet saith.
Whether man's heart or life it be
    which yields
    Thee harvest, must Thy harvest-fields
    Be dunged with rotten death?

  Now of that long pursuit
  Comes on at hand the bruit;
 That Voice is round me like a
    bursting sea:
   "And is thy earth so marred,
   Shattered in shard on shard?
  Lo, all things fly thee, for thou fliest Me!
   Strange, piteous, futile thing!
Wherefore should any set thee love apart?
Seeing none but I makes much of naught"
    (He said),
"And human love needs human meriting:
  How hast thou merited —
Of all man's clotted clay the dingiest clot?
  Alack, thou knowest not
How little worthy of any love thou art!
Whom wilt thou find to love ignoble thee
  Save Me, save only Me?
All which I took from thee I did but take,
  Not for thy harms,
But just that thou might'st seek it
    in My arms
  All which thy child's mistake
Fancies as lost, I have stored for thee
    at home:

Rise, clasp My hand, and come! "

Halts by me that footfall:
Is my gloom, after all,
Shade of His hand, outstretched
      caressingly?
"Ah, fondest, blindest, weakest,
I am He Whom thou seekest!
Thou dravest love from thee,
      who dravest Me."

— Francis Thompson

Once a year the roebuck, a musk-deer of the mountains, is haunted by the odor of scented perfume. He does not know where this odor comes from, but it is like the call of the flute of Khrishma which no one can resist.

Then the deer races from one area of the forest to another in pursuit of the scent. The poor animal gives up food, drink, sleep and everything else. Just as a child searches after an echo, calling after it on one side of the ravine, while the echo responds on the other, then crosses the ravine and hears on that side the cry that responds to it, so does the deer. He does not know where the scent comes from, but he is compelled to go after it across ravines, forests and hills until at last hungry, weary, in fact exhausted, he wanders aimlessly, slips from the top of a rock and falls to his death, broken in body and spirit.

His last act before dying is to take pity on himself and to lick himself .,. but wait, the perfume had developed on his own body. He pants deeply, trying to inhale the perfume, but it is too late.

— O my beloved son, do not look outside of yourself for the sweet fragrance of God, to perish sooner or later in the jungle of life, but rather look within your soul, and behold, He will be there. Do not cease to search for Him within yourself, no matter how strongly the senses try to prove that He, like a deceptive echo, is outside of you.

UNCERTAIN EVIDENCE

When the ducks and wild geese come forth when it is time to migrate, a strange tide is seen in the regions when they are in great number. The domestic birds, as if magnetized by the great triangular flight, attempt an awkward flight and fall to earth in a short while. The call of the wild evokes in them, with the force of a harpoon, some wild trait. And now the farm ducks are transformed for a minute into migratory birds. In that small, hard head of theirs, where small images of tides, worms and hens whirl about, there spring visions of continental distances, the taste for sea winds and the vast expanse of oceans. And the duck staggers from left to right in his fenced-in enclosure, caught by this sudden passion which will lead it to unknown regions and by this vast love whose object he will never know.

Likewise, man, gripped by evidence he is uncertain of, discovers the emptiness of his business interests as well as the pleasures of his domestic life. But he does not know what name to give to this sovereign truth. . .

This call that has disturbed you torments all men, no doubt. . . . But domestic tranquility has choked off the part in us that could hear it. We take a short jump, flap our wings two or three times, and fall down into our court yard. We are rational beings. We are afraid of letting go of our tiny conquests for the sake of a huge shadow...

The domestic duck did not know his little head was large enough to contain oceans, continents, skies, but here he is, flapping his wings, refusing the grain, scorning the worms, and wanting to become a wild duck...

Some migratory birds take off over the ocean amid unfavorable winds. And the ocean becomes too immense for their flight, and they no longer know if they will reach the other side. But in their head remain images of the sun that fortify them in their flight.

... When the day comes when the eels must return to the Sargasso Sea, you cannot hold them back. They scorn the comfort and calm of warm waters. They go their own way, tear themselves in the bay, flay themselves on rocks. They seek the river, which will bring them to the unfathomed depths.

> — Antoine de Saint-Exupéry, *Un sens à la vie* (Gallimard, 1956), p. 138

I Went Out after Thee, Calling, and Thou Wert Gone.

There can be no medicine for the wounds of love save that which comes from him that dealt the wounds. For this cause the soul says that she went out calling — that is, after Him that had wounded her — begging for medicine and crying out at the violence of the burning that was caused by the wound... 'And Thou wert gone.'

As though she had said: At the time when I desired to possess Thy presence I found Thee not, and for Thy sake I remained empty and detached from all things, and yet I bound not myself to Thee; I was buffeted woefully by the gales of love and found support neither in myself nor in Thee. . .

This affliction and sorrow for the absence of God is wont to be so great in those that are approaching ever nearer to perfection, at the time of these Divine wounds, that, if the Lord provided not for them, they would die.

> — St. John of the Cross, *Spiritual Canticle*, Stanza I, in *The Complete Works of Saint John of the Cross, op. cit.*, vol. II

GOING AS FAR AS ONE CAN

The only thing to do is to go as far as one can. You have prayed, wept, sighed, groaned. But have you fasted, stayed up late, slept on the ground or scourged yourself? As long as you have not gone this far, do not think that you have done everything.

The good Lord gives me almost everything I ask, except when I pray for myself.

Man is capable of two kinds of crying: the cry of the angel and the cry of the beast. The cry of the angel is prayer; the cry of the beast is sin. Those who do not pray descend into the earth, like a mole trying to find a hole to hide himself. They are wholly terrestrial, stupefied, and think only of transitory things. They resemble the beggar who was being ministered to: when a silver crucifix was given to him so that he might kiss it, he said, "There's a crucifix that weighs a good ten ounces."

God holds on to the interior man like a
woman holding her child's head in her hands in
order to cover it with kisses and caresses. People
like something in proportion to the price that
must be paid; on this account, consider the love
that our Lord has for us and which cost him all
his blood. For this reason, God yearns to communicate with us and to enter into a relationship
with us.

— Curé of Ars

There is no doubt, Lord Jesus, that you want
something from me. All those doors opened at
once! The one that lies before me — this life —
is no longer a dream.

You want something from me, Lord. Here I
am at the base of a wall; everything is open,
there is but one way, leading toward the infinite,
the absolute.

And yet I feel the same, despite everything. I
must make contact with you, Lord, and stay with
you for a very long time. In order to die, but
then completely.

Like those who are wounded and who suffer,
Lord, I ask you to bring me through to the end.
I am tired of not being Yours, of not being You.

— *Carnet de route de Jean Ploussard*
(Ed. du Seuil, 1964), p. 209

What would they do, my God, all those poor
things that do not subsist,

If, by their nature which is to come forth and
to cease, they did not bear witness that you are
here and there?

How would things have a meaning if their
meaning was not to pass on?

If the world did not speak so much of you, my disappointment would not be such.

Things are leaving me little by little, and I in turn leave them.

One can only enter, exposed, into the councils of Love.

My God, I offer you this great desire to exist;

My God, I offer you this great desire to avoid chance and appearance!

In the Love that is my end, face to face, in the Cause that is truth,

There only shall I find my abode.

— Paul Claudel, *La messe là-bas*

O God, Father, in my innermost being be my majority.

— Emmanuel Mounier

GIVE ME MY BROTHERS

Lord God, here is my life so that you may do what you want with it. But you cannot prevent the fact that wherever you will send me, happy or in grief, sick or in good health, enthusiastic or humiliated, the Spirit in me will clamor vehemently after you, calling imperiously for your Love for my brothers, who do not know that you are a Father.

O Father, here is my life, but give me my brothers so that I may give them back to you.

— Père Lyonnet, *Ecrits spirituels*

It is not enough for me to love God, if my neighbor does not love him.

— St. Vincent de Paul

Lord, my God! You, the Creator, you, the Master, you who have made the Law and freedom; you, the Sovereign, who lets men do what they want, you, the judge, who grants pardon, you who are filled with motives and causes, and who have perhaps instilled in my spirit the taste for honor in order to convert my heart, like the recovery at the end of a wave. Lord, have pity, have pity on fools, both men and women! O Creator! Can there exist monsters in the eyes of Him alone who knows why they exist, how they *are made* and how they could *not be made*?

> — Charles Baudelaire, "Prière pour les fous," in *Mademoiselle Bistouri* (Ed. de la Pleiade), p. 352

I went begging from door to door on the village road when your golden chariot appeared in the distance, like a splendid dream, and I wondered who was this king of all kings!

My hopes increased, and I thought, "The bad days are over," and I was ready in the hope of spontaneous alms and riches scattered everywhere in the dust.

The chariot stopped where I was standing. Your glance fell upon me and you got down, smiling. I felt that the great moment of my life had finally come. Then, suddenly, you extended your right hand and said: "What do you have to give me?"

What royal game was this, extending your hand to a beggar in order to beg! I was confused and remained perplexed. Finally, from my sack, I slowly drew a small grain of wheat and gave it to you.

But how great was my surprise when at the end of the day I emptied my sack and found a small grain of gold amid the pile of meager grains. I wept bitterly, and then thought "Why didn't I have the heart to give you my whole self? "

GIVING GOD TO GOD

. . . And in this way, since the soul, by means of this substantial transformation, is the shadow of God, it does in God and through God that which He does through Himself in the soul, in the same way as He does it. For the will of these two is one; and, even as God is giving Himself to the soul with free and gracious will, even so likewise the soul, having a will that is the freer and the more generous in proportion as it has a greater degree of union with God, is giving God in God to God Himself, and thus the gift of the soul to God is true and entire. For in this state the soul truly sees that God belongs to it, and that it possesses him with hereditary possession, as an adopted child of God, by rightful ownership, through the grace that God gave to it of Himself, and it sees that, since He belongs to it, it may give and communicate Him to whomsoever it desires; and thus it gives Him to its Beloved, Who is the very God that gave Himself to it. And herein the soul pays all that it owes; for, of its own will, it gives as much as it has received with inestimable delight and joy, giving to the Holy Spirit that which is His in a voluntary surrender, that He may be loved as He deserves.

And herein is the inestimable delight of the soul: to see that it is giving to God that which is His own and which becomes Him according to His infinite Being. For, although it is true that the soul cannot give God Himself to Himself anew, since He in Himself is ever Himself, yet, in so far as the soul is itself concerned, it gives perfectly and truly, giving all that He had given to it, to pay the debt of love. And this is to give as has been given to it, and God is repaid by that gift of the soul — yet with less than this He cannot be paid... And so at this time there is a reciprocal love between God and the soul ... wherein each says to the other that which the Son of God said to the Father in St. John, namely: *Omnia mea tua sunt, et tua mea sunt et clarificatus sum in eis* [John 17:10]. That is: All My things are Thine, and Thine are Mine, and I am glorified in them.

> — St. John of the Cross, *Living Flame of Love*, Stanza III, in *The Complete Works of Saint John of the Cross, op. cit.*, vol. III

KNOWING GOD LOVES US

If only we knew how our Lord loves us, we would die from joy! I do not think there exist hearts hard enough not to love when they realize they are loved so much... The only happiness we have on earth, is loving God and knowing that God loves us.

Everything in the sight of God, everything with God, everything to please God. Oh, how wonderful that is! Come, my soul! You are going to talk with the good God, work with him, walk with him, fight and suffer with him. You shall work, but he will bless your work; you shall walk, but he will bless your steps; you shall suffer, but he will bless your tears. Doing everything together and in the sight of the good God! Realizing that he sees everything, that he keeps track of everything! Let us, therefore, say each morning: Everything to please you, my God! All my acts done with you! Never will we grow tired, the hours will pass like minutes... In other words, a foretaste of heaven.

Poor sinners! When I think that there are some who will die without having tasted for only an hour the happiness of loving God! If a person could damn himself without causing our Lord to suffer, well and good! But that is impossible!

> – Curé of Ars, as cited in Monnin, *op. cit.*, t. II, p. 412

BECOME IN ME THE DAY

Serene light of my soul, Morning ablaze with the sweetest of fires, become in me the day. Love that not only enlightens but makes divine, come to me with your power, sweetly dissolve all my being. Destroyed insofar as I am myself, let me pass completely into you.

It is you who loved me first; it is you who chose me. You are the one who rushes toward the creature; and the brilliance of eternal light shines on your forehead. Show me your face, all glimmering with the flames of the divine sun. Love, why did you love me, who am a creature and defiled, unless because you wanted to make me beautiful in you? Love, you who are God, without you heaven and earth would offer me no hope or desire: grant that your light may be my goal, the consummation of my being. In the traces of my God, your light shines like the evening star; at the hour of my death, show me your rays.

Beloved Evening, let me sleep in you in peaceful sleep and taste this happy repose that you have prepared in yourself for those whom you love.

— St. Gertrude

CLOTHE ME WITH YOURSELF

Eternal Trinity, you are a bottomless ocean, wherein the deeper I plunge the better I find you, and the better I find you, the more I look for you. Of you, it can never be said: that's enough! The soul that fills itself in your depths, desires you unceasingly since it always hungers for you, eternal Trinity; it always desires to see the light in your light. Just as a stag longs for the fresh water of the springs, so my soul wishes to come forth from the dark prison of the body, to really see you! . . .

Can you give me more than you give yourself? You are the flame that ever burns and is never extinguished! You are the flame that consumes all the self-love of the soul; you are the light beyond all light. . .

You are the raiment that covers all nudity, the nourishment that delights, with its sweetness, all those who are hungry. For you are sweet, and without a trace of bitterness!

Clothe me, eternal Trinity, clothe me with yourself so that I may spend this mortal life in true obedience and in the light of a very holy faith, with which you have intoxicated my soul.

— *Le dialogue de Sainte Cathérine de Sienne*, trans. J. Hurtaud (Ed. Lethielleux, 1947), t. II, p. 327

O my God, Trinity whom I adore, help me to forget myself completely so that I may remain in you.

. . . Christ, my beloved, crucified by love, I sense my lack of power and ask you to cover me with yourself, to identify my soul with all the movements of your soul; to substitute yourself for me so that my life may be but the resplendence of your life. Come to me as Adorer, as Restorer and as Saviour.

. . . Consuming Fire, Spirit of love, remain in me so that an incarnation of the Word, so to speak, may take place in my soul; so that I may be for Him a new humanity in which he might renew all his mystery.

And you, Father, lean toward your creature; see in it the Beloved in whom you are satisfied.

O Three Persons, my all, my beatitude, infinite solitude, immensity in which I lose myself, I surrender to you as a kind of prey; bury yourself in me so that I might become buried in you, before I may contemplate in your light the depths of your grandeur.

— Sister Elizabeth of the Trinity

NOT FOR HIS GIFTS

It is not for his gifts
that I continue in my prayers,
but because he is true Life.

It is not so much by hope
as by bonds of love that I am drawn.
It is not for gifts,
but for the Giver that I ever yearn.

It is not glory I aspire to,
but it is the Glorified One whom I wish to
  embrace.
It is not by the desire for life,
but by the remembrance of Him who
  gives life
that I am ever consumed!

It is not for joyous passions that I yearn,
but it is because of a desire for Him who
  is preparing them
that my heart bursts out in tears.
It is not rest that I seek,
but it is the face of Him who offers rest
that I seek in prayer.

It is not for the nuptial banquet,
but it is for the Bridegroom that I long.
Despite the weight of my transgressions
I believe with an indubitable hope,
trusting in the hand of the Almighty One
that not only shall I obtain pardon,
but that I shall see him in person,
thanks to his mercy and pity,
and that I shall inherit heaven
although I completely deserve to be banished.

. . . Receive with sweetness,
  O powerful Lord God,
the prayer of him who was bitterness
  for You.
. . . Grant that through remembrance of
  your hope
I may remain unscathed, protected by
  You. Amen.

> — St. Gregory of Narek, *Le Livre des
> Prières*, trans. J. Kechichian (Ed. du
> Cerf, 1961), p. 102

ASKING FOR SUFFERING, BUT UNABLE TO BEAR IT

O my Lord Jesu, I believe, and by Thy grace will ever believe and hold, and I know that it is true, and will be true to the end of the world, that nothing great is done without suffering, without humiliation, and that all things are possible by means of it. I believe, O my God, that poverty is better than riches, pain better than pleasure, obscurity and contempt than name, and ignominy and reproach than honour. My Lord, I do not ask Thee to bring these trials on me, for I know not if I could face them; but at least, O Lord, whether I be in prosperity or adversity, I will believe that it is as I have said. I will never have faith in riches, rank, power, or reputation. I will never set my heart on worldly success or on worldly advantages. I will never wish for what men call the prizes of life. I will ever, with Thy grace, make much of those who are despised or neglected, honour the poor, revere the suffering, and admire and venerate Thy saints and confessors, and take my part with them in spite of the world.

And lastly, O my dear Lord, though I am so very weak that I am not fit to ask Thee for suffering as a gift, and have not strength to do so, at least I will beg of Thee grace to meet suffering well, when Thou in Thy love and wisdom dost bring it upon me.

> — John Henry Newman, "The Power of the Cross", *Meditations on Christian Doctrine.*

YOU ARE OUR ETERNAL LIFE

You are holy, Lord God, you alone who work miracles. You are strong. You are great. You are on high. You are all-powerful king, holy Father, king of heaven and earth. You are three and one, Lord God, all good. You are goodness, all goodness, the sovereign goodness, the living and true Lord God. You are charity, love. You are wisdom. You are humility. You are patience. You are assurance. You are quietude. You are joy and gaiety. You are justice and temperance. You are all wealth and our sufficiency. You are beauty. You are calm. You are protector. You are guardian and defender. You are strength. You are refreshment. You are our hope. You are our faith. You are our great sweetness. You are our eternal life, great and admirable Lord, God almighty, merciful Saviour.

> — St. Francis of Assisi, *Opuscules de Saint François* (Ed. Franciscaines, 1945), p. 171

The love of God for man —
it is that God makes himself
his own test.

> — Al Hallaj

CONCLUSION

DIVINE ASSISTANCE FOR OUR PRAYER

". . . always living to make intercession for us."

— HEBREW 7:25

INCARNATION OR ESCHATOLOGY?

IT is impossible to avoid the accomplices God gives us in our life, in the sense that St. Vincent de Paul spoke of the poor as "accomplices of God." In the case of prayer, we can cite three: our weakness and our own limitations, other people, events. In each instance, something is seriously lacking as long as we do not inform God, through our prayer, about our selves and our lives. Moreover, we do not find a solution by only going half way, but by going through all of the requirements of such cooperation.

Discovering our Limitations

Prayer sometimes occasions a false kind of fear, i.e., fear of asking for something. Every prayer includes recognizing the fact that we need something. As we have already remarked, leaving behind one's adolescence is accomplished only by a person's discovering and accepting his limitations and lack of strength. At that point, a man finds out that he needs God far more than he realized. As a result of prayer, he can transform, through a new kind of life, the very thing that is over-powering him. Fatigue, lack of drive, loneliness or promiscuity, sin itself, everything that tends to separate us from God can give rise to prayer, by encouraging us to ask for what we need.

But asking for something can also arise from impure motives. Rather than fearing this, we should go through a learning process. Every method of prayer revolves around such a learning process, which is characterized by hope, and which cannot be achieved without the help of Christ. We will learn that a genuine request can be made only if we have discovered whom it is we are addressing. "Our Father..." It is to the Father of our Lord Jesus Christ that we pray, and precisely because he is the Father who has given us Christ. An act of thanksgiving, therefore, precedes our request. Since he has already given us his son, we can be sure of him, and since this gift reveals his power and mercy, it is right and just that we adore him — for himself alone.

In this way will our prayer be truly Christian. Never separating the three elements — thanksgiving, adoration, petition — our request will pay homage to the gratuitousness that made it possible, in the name of Christ, and will thereby find its justification.

Discovering other Men

Every life lived in association with other people soon makes clear our inability to really respect and love our neighbor simply by means of our own resources. It is actually impossible without recourse to God, whereby we may overcome our limitations. Life puts our neighbor before us: Shall I follow a new road in order not to see him? Without a prayer of petition, who can claim that he loves this neighbor, since it is difficult to love oneself without the aid of prayer?

This other person is appointed by God to bring out the best in us, to give birth to what is divine within us, perhaps against our will. That is why he can become a sign of God and his accomplice. The purpose of all prayer is not different from that of charity: to realize the Father's will, which, for us, is to love one another as he loves us and to be brothers since he is the Father. "Thy will be done on earth as it is in heaven."

But a man's neighbor has another role. Not only does he oblige us to ask for help in view of a new impossibility — respecting and assuring his existence — but he teaches us, little by little, what "someone else" is, and above all that God is not merely someone else, simply another man, with respect to us. Together with the training involved in making a request, the training involved in otherness is the key to the apprenticeship required for true prayer. All of our mistakes in prayer come from the fact that we treat God like another man. While dependency upon another person is involved, this Other Person enjoys an extremely special position: he ranks high above me and always an extremely special position: he ranks high above me and always anticipates what I ask. "Where were you when I founded the earth?" God asked Job. And Job could not answer. But one thing changes everything: God reserved a place for me in his plans a long time ago, because of a feeling of love.

Events

Hamlet complained that he was unable to anticipate his future. But who among us today does not experience anxiety at one time or another in the face of future events?

Must a person opt for the absurd and the irrational because a horizontal look is not enough to situate ourselves? On the other hand, what is hidden and resists our look in a particular event is perhaps an opportunity given by God to get a better view of him, one that is infinitely different than I had had and yet one that is infinitely more intimate. A god who is, as it were, too far away or else too close is not a god to whom one prays very much. An event can recall to us that man is not master of the immediate situation, which is actually more overwhelming that he had thought! "God be with us!"

To be "co-workers with God!" This is what is suggested by every event: to be able to set in motion, as the result of prayer, a divine force. God wanted us to intervene in what he did and to invest us with his own omnipotence since he assigned a place for us in his plans and left hanging in the balance some part of the world's salvation which depends on our intervention.

Incarnation or eschatology? Transcendence of faith or the problem of man? We would not be honest if we did not recognize this tension in the life of every Christian and if we did not heed both calls of the same Spirit.

But the transfiguration of an event is possible only as the result of a struggle. Job, together with all of those whom God has loved, showed us that this struggle is far different from the struggles we have on earth. It is a "struggle with the angel," that is with all the strength of the spirit and the passions. The servant cannot hope to complete his journey differently than the way his Master did. The agony with an angel precedes every passover. But the servant knows that every day thereafter the slightest utterance of prayer is of infinite value since he is no longer alone in offering it to God.

APPENDIX

THE GREAT PRAYERS
OF THE OLD TESTAMENT

Genesis	18:16-33	Abraham intercedes for Sodom.
	24	Eliezer seeks a wife for Isaac.
	32:10-13	Jacob returns from exile.
Exodus	15	The song of Moses after the Red Sea.
	32:11-34:9	Moses prays for the people.
Numbers	14:13-19	Moses prays for the people.
I Samuel	1:9-15 2:1-11	Anna, mother of Samuel.
II Samuel	7:18-29	David, after he has learned of God's choice.
I Kings	8:1-53	Dedication of the Temple.
	18:36-37	Elias at the moment of sacrifice.
II Kings	19:14-19	Ezechias, for deliverance.
I Chronicles	16:8-36	(II Samuel 7:18-29).
	17:16-27	David, on the promise of God.
	29:10-20	David, prayer for Solomon.
II Chronicles	20:5-13	Josaphat, before the invasion.
Esdras	9	Esdras, for the confession of sins.
II Macchabees	1:18-36	Nehemias, for the renewal of the sacred fire.

Wisdom	9:1-18	Solomon, for wisdom.
Ecclesiastes	36:1-17	For deliverance.
	51:1-12	Act of thanksgiving.
Tobias	3:1-6	Prayer of Tobias.
	3:11-15	Prayer of Sara.
	8:4-8	Prayer of Tobias and Sara.
	13:1-17	Song of Tobias.
Judith	(4:9-15)	The great prayers of the people.
	6:14-21	
	7:19-29	God is not a son of man.
	8:10-27	
	9:1-14	The God of the humble.
Esther	(4:17a-k)	Prayer of Mardochea
	(4:17k-z)	Prayer of Esther
Isaiah	38:1-20	Ezechias, before death.
	63:7-64:11	Prayer of the people.
Jeremias	17:12-18	Confidence and vengeance.
	20:7-13	Confessions.
	32:17-25	Power of God.
Lamentations	5	Remember, Yahweh.
Baruch	2:11-3:8	Prayer of the exiled.
Daniel	3:26-45	Song of Azaria
	3:52-90	Song of the three young men.
Jonas	2:3:10	Saving of Jonas.
Habacuc	3:1-19	Remember, Yahweh.

PRAYER IN THE NEW TESTAMENT

A. THE EXAMPLE OF CHRIST

Movements of His prayer

Luke	3:21	After baptism.
Mark	1:35	At the end of the first day of miracles at Capharnaum.
Luke	6:12	Before the choice of the Twelve.
Mark	6:46	Conclusion of the multiplication of the loaves of bread.

Luke	9:18	Before the confession of Caesarea.
Luke	9-28	Before the Transfiguration.
Luke	11:1	Before the teaching of the *Our Father*.
John	11:41-42	Before the resurrection of Lazarus.
Luke	22:32	Before Peter's denial.

His Prayers

Luke	11:1-4	The *Our Father*.
Luke	10:21	Thanksgiving of Christ before the revelation of which he is bearer.
Matthew	11:25-26	Thanksgiving of Christ before the revelation of which he is bearer.
Matthew	6:26-28	The Eucharist.
John	17	The *Priestly Prayer*, which gives meaning to his Passion.
Mark	14:32-36	Prayer at the Agony at Gethsemane.
Luke	23:34	Prayer for the executioners.
Mark	15:34	Prayer of abandonment and total remission.
Matthew	27:46	*In manus tuas*.
Luke	23:46	*In manus tuas*.
Luke	5:12-14	The lepers.
Matthew	8:5-13	The centurion of Capharnaum.
Luke	7:21	The messengers of John the Baptist.
Luke	7:48	The sinful woman.
Mark	14:37-39	The Apostles terrified by the stom.
Luke	8:40,49,50	Jairus.
Luke	8:43-48	The woman suffering from a hemorrhage.
John	5:5-8	The infirm man at the pool of Bethsaida.
Matthew	15:22-28	The Chanaanite woman.

Mark	7:32-35	The deaf and dumb man.
Mark	8:22-25	The blind man at Bethsaida.
Luke	17:14	The ten lepers.
Mark	10:50-52	The blind man at Jericho.
Luke	23:42-43	The good thief.

Interior Supplication

Luke	5:20	The paralytic at Capharnaum.
Luke	6:10	The man with a withered hand.
Luke	7:13-14	The widow of Naim.
John	8:11	The adulterous woman.
John	9:6-7	The man born blind.
Luke	19:3-6	Zachaeus in the sycamore tree.
John	12:7	Mary of Bethany anointing with perfume.

Prayers Unanswered

Mark	9:5	Peter desires to set up tents on the mountain.
Luke	9:59-60	A disciple wishes to bury someone.
Luke	9:61-62	A disciple wants to bid farewell to his family.
Luke	10:40-42	Martha wants Jesus to ask Mary to help her.
Matthew	20:20	The mother of James and John.

B. THE TEACHING OF OUR LORD AND THE APOSTLES

Pray like a Poor Man (in the desire for the Face of God and in expectation of the Kingdom)

| Luke | 18:9-14 | The Pharisee and the Publican. |
| Matthew | 25:1-13 | Parable of the virgins. |

Mark	13:33-37	Be vigilant.
Matthew	24:43-50	At a time when you do not expect it.
I Thessalonians	5:2-6	Let us not fall asleep.
I Corinthians	16:22	"Lord, come."
Apocalypse	22:20	My return is close at hand.

Pray at Every Opportunity ("continually" — "always" — "unceasingly")

Luke	18:1 ff.	Parable of the unjust judge.
Luke	11:5-8	Parable of the importunate friend.
Luke	11:9-13	Efficaciousness of prayer.
Matthew	7:7	Ask, seek, knock.
Philippians	4:6	In every need.
Ephesians	5:20	At every moment.
Acts	1:14	Complete steadfastness in prayer.
	12:5	Without respite.
	6:6	For the institution of deacons.
	13:3	For missionary work.
	20:7-11	Until daybreak.
	10:2	Unceasingly.
	16:25	Towards midnight, in prayer.

Pray in the Name of Jesus: In the Spirit

John	14:13	What you will ask in my name.
John	16:23-24	He will give it to you in my name.
John	11:41-42	You always hear me.
Romans	8:33-34	He who intercedes for us.
Colossians	3:16-17	Always in the name of the Lord.

Ephesians	3:11-12	Draw near in all confidence.
Philippians	2:5	The sentiments of Jesus in you.
Hebrews	9:14	He who offered himself.
Hebrews	7:25	Living always to make intercession.
I John	2:1	Our advocate.
Apocalypse	5:4-10	The slain Lamb is alone worthy to open the book.
II Corinthians	1:20	Through him the Amen is pronounced for us.
Luke	11:13	Your Father will give the Holy Spirit.
Ephesians	5:20	Give thanks in the name of our Saviour, Jesus Christ.
	6:18	Pray at all times in the Spirit. . .
I Corinthians	14:15	I will pray by the Spirit.
Romans	8:26	The Spirit himself intercedes.
I Corinthians	12:3	No one says, Jesus, except by the Spirit.
Galatians	4:6	The Spirit of his Son, who cries, Abba.

C. THE ATTITUDE OF OUR LORD TOWARD THOSE WHO PRAY

John	2:1-12	The Virgin at Cana.
John	4:1-26	The Samaritan woman.
John	4:46-50	The dignitary at Capharnaum.
Mark	1:29-31	The Apostles imploring the cure of St. Peter's mother-in-law.

THE PRAYER OF THE LITURGY

CYCLE OF CHRISTMAS

*"The Word was with God . . . and
was the light of men."*

Advent	Isaiah	The *waiting* of the people *Promise of a Saviour* Certitude and confidence in Almighty God.
Christmas	Epistle to the Romans	The *manifestation of love* freeing us from anger, sin, death.
Epiphany	Synoptic Gospels	The manifestation of *Christ the Lord:* Saviour, Master, Judge.

CYCLE OF EASTER, PENTECOST

"The darkness did not comprehend it, but to all those who received him he gave power to become the sons of God."

Septuagesima Passion	{ Genesis Exodus Epistles of Captivity	{ The history of *Salvation*, its reasons.
Passion Palm Sunday	{ Job Jeremias Isaiah 52, 53	{ The *suffering servant*.
Passion Easter Sunday Period after Easter	{ St. John (Gospel, Epistles, Apocalypse)	{ The mysteries of the *risen* Saviour The new life Waiting for the Spirit of love.
Pentecost	{ Acts of the Apostles	{ Founding of the Church.
Period after Pentecost	{ Synoptic Gospels Historical Books of the Old Testament	{ Nature of the future Kingdom Its history Its laws.
	{ The Prophets Wisdom Books	{ God acting in him Waiting for the judgment The Parousia, final Kingdom.

PRAYER FROM THE PSALMS

I

THE PSALMS AS PRAYERS OF CHRIST*

Christ Made Man:

His vocation: 2, 88, 109, 131.
His entrance into the world: 18, 39.
His life, his dialogue with the Father: 2, 4, 20, 30, 33, 41,
62, 83, 85, 90, 118, 138.

The Passion:

Christ as Saviour: 6, 9, 31, 36.
Christ and sin: 6, 9, 50, 72.
Christ crucified: 21, 68, 87.

Glorified Christ:

Victorious: 17, 75, 117, 123.
His Ascension: 23, 26, 44, 46, 109.
Judge: 45, 57, 74, 81, 93, 149.
His reign: 2, 71, 92, 94, 95, 96, 98, 99, 100.

THE PSALMS AS PRAYERS OF THE CHURCH

Birth of the Church — Its Life:

Foundation and confirmation: 45, 47, 67, 86, 147.
Its history: as type: 77, 104, 105, 106.
as revelation: 80, 84.
Its pilgrimage: 65, 83, 120, 121, 124-126, 128, 130, 136.
Its prayer: 65, 70, 76, 94, 129, 134.

---

* The numbers of the Psalms listed here refer to the numbers used
in the Vulgate edition, and which are placed in parentheses in
the Bible.

The Church and Salvation:

> Penitent: 36, 43, 48, 54, 59, 73, 129.
> Missionary Church: 66, 86, 95.
> The Church of martyrs: 63, 78, 79.
> Its exile: 125, 136.
> Peace and unity: 45, 67, 83, 132, 146.

The Church in the Glory:

> Its act of thanksgiving: 64-67, 106, 112-117, 123, 128, 134-137, 144-150.
> The Church and the praise of creation: 8, 18, 23, 28, 64, 103, 148.

THE PSALMS AS PRAYERS OF THE VIRGIN MARY

Immaculate Conception: 17, 29, 65, 92.
Annunciation: 44.
Christmas: 18, 23, 86.
Suffering with her Son: 12, 30, 37, 38, 139, 142.
Assumption: 44, 45, 83, 86.

II

IN THE LITURGICAL YEAR

Advent: 18, 24, 79, 84.
Christmas-Epiphany: 2, 18, 28, 46, 65, 71, 92, 94, 95, 99.
Lent and Passion: 6, 29, 31, 37, 42, 50, 101, 129, 142.
Good Friday: 21, 58, 68, 87.
Holy Saturday: 15, 29.
Easter: 65, 75, 112, 113, 117, 138.
Ascension: 26, 46.
Pentecost: 47, 66, 103; etc.

IN THE SACRAMENTS AND STAGES OF LIFE

Baptism: 1, 22, 41, 77, 104, 113, 117.
Penance: temptation: 4, 21, 68, 90.
  contrition: 6, 31, 37, 50, 101, 129.
  purification: 11, 29, 34, 36, 50, 53.
  pardon: 102, 112, 114, 115.

ON ALL OCCASIONS

SELECTED EXAMPLES OF PSALMS
USED IN THE NEW TESTAMENT

PSALM 2 : v.2 : Acts 4:25-27
    v.7 : Acts 13:33
    v.9 : Apocalypse 2:27

PSALM 6 : v.4 : John 12:27

PSALM 8 : v.3 : Matthew 21:16
    v.5 : Hebrews 2:6
    v.7 : Hebrews 2:7-8
       I Corinthians 15:27

PSALM 15 : v.9 : Acts 2:26
       I Thessalonians 4:13
    : v.10 : Acts 2:27-31
       Acts 13:35-37

PSALM 21 : v.2 : Matthew 27-46
       Mark 15:34
    v.9 : Matthew 27:43
    v.19 : John 19:24
    v.23 : Hebrews 2:12

PSALM 23 : v.1 : I Corinthians 10:26

PSALM 33 : v.13-16 : I Peter 3:10-12
    v.8 : I Peter 2:3
    v.21 : John 19:36

PSALM 34 : v.19 : John 15:25

PSALM 37 : v.11-12 : Luke 23:49

PSALM 39 : v.9-11 : Hebrews 10:5-10

PSALM 40 : v.10 : John 13:18

PSALM 41 : v.6 : Matthew 26:38

PSALM 44 : v.8-9 : Hebrews 1:8-9

PSALM 49 : v.15 : Hebrews 13:15

INDEX

For those who would like to make a more analytical study of prayer, or to simply locate a particular paragraph, the following Index lists the page numbers containing the more important concepts discussed in this book.